TALES OF TOMORROW: TELEVISION'S FIRST SCIENCE FICTION SERIES FOR ADULTS

TALES OF TOMORROW: TELEVISION'S FIRST SCIENCE FICTION SERIES FOR ADULTS

RICHARD IRVIN

BearManor Media
2023

Tales of Tomorrow: Television's First Science Fiction Series for Adults

This book is an independent work of research and commentary and is not sponsored, authorized or endorsed by, or otherwise affiliated with, any motion picture studio or production company affiliated with the films discussed herein. All uses of the name, image, and likeness of any individuals, and all copyrights and trademarks referenced in this book, are for editorial purposes and are pursuant of the Fair Use Doctrine.

The views and opinions of individuals quoted in this book do not necessarily reflect those of the author.

The promotional photographs and publicity materials reproduced herein are in the author's private collection (unless noted otherwise). These images date from the original release of the films and were released to media outlets for publicity purposes.

Published in the USA by
BearManor Media
1317 Edgewater Dr. #110
Orlando, FL 32804
www.BearManorMedia.com

Hardcover Edition
ISBN: 979-8-88771-306-9

Printed in the United States of America

Table of Contents

Acknowledgements

The author would like to thank the following institutions and individuals for their help with this book:

Wisconsin Center for Film and Theater Research for script copies from the Reginald Rose Papers and the Rod Serling Papers;

Marshall University Library Special Collections for copies of scripts from the Nelson Bond Papers;

The Writers Guild Foundation for information about various *Tales of Tomorrow* scripts it holds;

Kenneth Spencer Research Library Archival Collections, University of Kansas, for information from the papers of Theodore Sturgeon;

Billy Rose Division, New York Public Library for documents from the Florence Anglin Papers;

Glen Sturgeon and the UCLA Film and Television Archive for details about two episodes of *Tales of Tomorrow* – "Homecoming" and "Ink;"

Syracuse University Libraries for information from the Murray Leinster Papers;

The American Heritage Center, University of Wyoming for copies of scripts from the Mann Rubin Papers and the Irwin Blacker Papers; and

Garry Settimi for assistance on editing the manuscript.

Tales of Tomorrow: The Television Series

Tales of Tomorrow, premiering August 3, 1951 on ABC, was an anthology that introduced viewers to tales of strange and surreal happenings using both contemporary and period stories. George F. Foley, Jr. and Mort Abrahams produced the series. *Tales of Tomorrow* presented a variety of science fiction and other speculative fiction stories similar to the later anthologies - *The Outer Limits* and Rod Serling's *The Twilight Zone.*

This book chronicles all the television episodes of the series and, where applicable, details the short stories that inspired them. It also describes the episodes for the short-lived radio version of the television series. In addition, there is a section about stories that were considered but never produced for the TV series, including one authored by Rod Serling. An appendix describes *Out There*, a science fiction show that CBS introduced as that network's answer to *Tales of Tomorrow.*

Science fiction is one type of speculative fiction that deals with scenarios that do not currently exist such as advanced robots, outer space aliens, time travel, mutants, and other manifestations of science run amok. Other types of speculative fiction include fantasy, horror, dystopian tales that take place in a highly problematic society, and apocalyptic and post-apocalyptic stories about the end of the world or the survivors of a worldwide cataclysm. While *Tales of Tomorrow* mainly presented science fiction stories, sometimes it aired horror, apocalyptic, and post-apocalyptic yarns.

Tales of Tomorrow was originally called *Tomorrow Is Yours.* In an interview with Jay Allen Sanford in May 1990, Mort Abrahams recalled that he put together a coalition of top science fiction writers like Ray Bradbury and Theodore Sturgeon to form the Science Fiction League of America.[1] The coalition gave him access to thousands of stories. The producers relied on such stories more for episodes from the first season and less for second season shows. In the second season, the series used many original scripts from writers like Mann Rubin and Frank De Felitta.

Mort Abrahams came to *Tales of Tomorrow* after producing the series *Tom Corbett, Space Cadet.* He would later help produce the anthology *General Electric Theater* as well as the spy series *The Man from U.N.C.L.E.* He was an associate producer for the film *Planet of the Apes* and the sequel, *Beneath the Planet of the Apes.*

Producer George F. Foley started his career as a lawyer before joining the Coast Guard as a combat correspondent. After being discharged, he tried advertising and helped to develop such shows as *Danger, Suspense,* and *Mr. I Magination.* He then became a package producer for television.

In speaking to *The New York Times* about the series, Foley opined that "The technique of our show is plain old suspense melodrama. Basically the story concerns both people and emotions in conflict. Our major problem is staging the scientific elements so they don't interfere with the basic human elements of the story. The science fiction part is the gimmick which makes it interesting to the audience."[2]

Tales of Tomorrow aired live on ABC each Friday at 9:30 pm from the network's New York City studio. Originally the series aired every other week alternating with ABC's *Versatile Varieties.* Several episodes of the series still exist because of the kinescope process which involved pointing a recording camera at a television set as the show aired, filming it for later broadcast to West Coast viewers. This book presents summaries of those episodes still available on kinescope. In cases, where the episode no longer exists, scripts or newspaper descriptions are used to describe the story line and cast of characters. Where a *Tales of Tomorrow* episode was based on a science fiction short story, that story is also summarized so readers can ascertain the differences between the TV installment and the story which inspired it.

Tales of Tomorrow was sponsored for most of its run by Jacques Kreisler Manufacturing Corporation, a maker of watch bands, and by Masland Carpets on alternating weeks. Robert F. Lewine, radio and television director of the Hirshon-Garfield Agency, an advertising agency, indicated four main reasons the series was broadcast live instead of being filmed:[3]

1. Film would deprive us of name appeal. Evidently, it was easier for top performers to be scheduled for a live show than for one on film. Related to this, stars would have to receive residuals for reruns of filmed episodes. Apparently, no one thought that the kinescopes of live presentations would ever be rerun.
2. Commercials would be frozen. The advertisers wanted live commercials, not ones on film. Lewine indicated that the seasonal nature of the products made it necessary to retain live commercials.
3. Time clearances would not be improved. The thinking was that if the series was on film, a network advertiser would pre-empt the advertising agency commercials in major television markets with multiple stations.
4. Sense of immediacy would be lost. The advertising agency was convinced that film would give the viewers less psychological immediacy.

Ironically, after *Tales of Tomorrow* was canceled by ABC, George Foley sought to make twenty-six half hour episodes filmed in color. The episodes would apparently have emphasized drama over outer space stories.[4]

Tales of Tomorrow was the first science fiction series aimed primarily at adults. Most previous science fiction shows on early TV were for youngsters. They included *Buck Rogers in the 25th Century* which ran on ABC from 1950 to 1951; *Captain Video and His Video*

Rangers which appeared on the DuMont Television network beginning in 1949; and *Space Patrol* that aired from 1950 to 1955.

However, prior to *Tales of Tomorrow,* there were some episodes of regular prime-time anthology series that fell into the category of science fiction stories aimed at adults.

17
"Colonel," said Joe, "I'd like to tell you, first of all, that this whole thing is a big—" The colonel wasn't listening. He was looking over at the shelves

An illustration of Joe McSween's Atomic Machine from *Collier's Weekly*.

The anthology, *The Actors Studio,* presented several fantasy and horror tales. The closest the series got to science fiction was an episode titled, "Joe McSween's Atomic Machine." The original story was written by Richard P. Gehman. Initially published in *Collier's Weekly* in December 1946, the tale focused on Joe McSween (Conrad Janis) and his buddy, Al Niles (James Stephens), who both live in Parkview U.S.A. and who, after military service, both got jobs at Turnball Fabrications – a plastic manufacturer. Joe is assigned to the X department, a top-secret project, where he works with a machine that is seven stories high. He works in front of an instrument panel, pressing a few buttons, turning some dials, and pulling a lever. He goes through the same motions every hour from 8:00 am to 5:00

pm. During his lunch hour, Al, who works in the shipping department, talks with Joe, who is frustrated with his job having no idea what the machine he runs actually does. Al tells him the machine is a fabricator but doesn't know what it fabricates. Joe would like to work at his old job where he could see the end product of his work. Al advises his friend not to quit since he is making more money at his job, enough so that he can marry his girlfriend Aggie (Nancy Franklin) someday.

To take his mind off the job, he starts to invent something telling his girlfriend that he will have to see her only two times a week instead of six times. Joe won't explain to anyone exactly what he is doing in his basement, but he does show his work to Al. Joe turns the machine on, and it begins to run with a great clanking of gears. The machine makes nothing; it just runs. Aggie, crouching by the cellar window, believes that her boyfriend has created a secret invention.

Joe wanted to construct a machine that he could control, instead of, like at work, a machine controlling him. Word spreads around town about Joe's invention. Not satisfied with Joe's answers about his creation, the local newspaper does an article about Joe's "atomic machine" as being the key to the universe.

The town council appropriates money for a statue of Joe's father holding Joe as an infant with the baby clutching a full-sized atom in his fist. The governor orders an investigation into Joe's creation and calls out the national guard to go to Joe's house and protect the top-secret machine. A National Guard lieutenant asks Joe for his documentation on his creation. Joe says he has none, it is all in his head. Joe attempts to explain what he created but instead just turns it on and lets it run. He then tries to smash the machine with a wrench, but the soldiers stop him.

Joe tries to convince Aggie that there is no atomic machine. He asks Al to explain to everyone that the machine was built only for his amusement and doesn't do anything. Nonetheless, Al now believes the machine has a secret purpose. He tells Joe that Turnball

Fabrications says that he can stay at home and work on his invention and still be paid his regular salary. When Joe responds that he doesn't know how to make an atomic anything, Al replies that Joe will learn. Aggie says that the entire nation will wait years if necessary.

The episode, adapted by Michael Zeamer from the short story titled "The Machine," initially aired March 6, 1949. The short story was later published in *13 Great Stories of Science Fiction* edited by Groff Conklin in 1960.

Lights Out, based on the radio series created by Wyllis Cooper, aired psychological dramas as well as episodes of speculative fiction. Some episodes presented science fiction stories.

The March 6, 1950 installment of *Lights Out* was based on a story, "The Strange Case of John Kingman," by Murray Leinster (Will Jenkins) which first appeared in *Astounding Science Fiction* in May 1948.

John Kingman has been institutionalized at Meadville Mental Hospital in Pennsylvania for several years. He has been diagnosed as paranoid and does not speak English. He also has six fingers on each hand. Dr. Braden takes over his care and inquires as to when Kingman was first admitted to the hospital. He eventually discovers that Kingman was first admitted in 1786 and so has been at the facility for 162 years.

The doctor wants to give Kingman a complete physical examination. While undergoing the examination, Kingman presents the X-ray technician with a drawing for an advanced X-ray machine. The doctor finds that his patient has two hearts and three extra ribs on each side.

Later, Kingman gives Braden a diagram showing a process to produce atomic energy. Braden concludes that his patient is not a human but an alien from outer space. Given Braden's findings and Kingman's knowledge of atomic energy, scores of scientists and psychiatrists descend on the hospital to study Kingman.

Braden tells the group that they cannot really trust what Kingman depicts for them since he is paranoid and regards humans as a lower life form. The doctor wants to give John Kingman experimental drug treatment. When Braden injects the drugs, Kingman begins having convulsions and is unconscious for three weeks. When he regains consciousness, he begins to talk and to learn English. He does not remember who he was and no longer has a superior attitude toward others. Also, he no longer recalls the secrets to atomic energy. He begins working in the hospital's records department and is perfectly happy.

Based on a story by science fiction writer Henry Kuttner titled "Don't Look Now," *Lights Out* aired "Martian Eyes" on October 30, 1950. Kuttner, born in Los Angeles in 1915, authored many stories in the 1940s and 1950s with his wife, C. L. Moore. Most of these stories were published under pseudonyms Lewis Padgett and Lawrence O'Donnell. In addition to this *Lights Out* episode, Kuttner stories were the basis for two episodes of *Tales of Tomorrow.*

"Martian Eyes" starred Burgess Meredith as Professor Lyman, researching Mars, who believes that a man in a bar is a Martian. He talks with a photographer at the bar named Sorrel (David Lewis) telling him that Martians hypnotize earthlings, want war on this planet, and have a third eye in the middle of their foreheads. The third eye can only be seen with infrared lighting. Sorrel is intrigued with Lyman's description of the third eye saying that, after developing a photo he took with an infrared camera, he saw such an eye on a person.

Sorrel invites the professor to his studio to view the photograph. Lyman phones Sorrel telling him that the man he claimed to be a Martian is following him but he thinks he shook him off. Nonetheless, the man shows up at Sorrel's studio. The man advises Sorrel that he wants Lyman committed to an institution for the mentally insane. While Sorrel is in his darkroom retrieving the photo he took, Lyman comes in and kills the man. Sorrel wants to make certain that the man was a Martian. Using infrared, he takes a photo of the dead man. When developed, there is no third eye. Sorrel tells Lyman that he made a mistake about the man. In the basement of the studio, Lyman has dug two graves – one for the dead man and one for Sorrel. The final scene shows Lyman with a third eye on his forehead.

The aforementioned Wyllis Cooper produced TV series presenting speculative fiction tales in the late 1940s and early 1950s including some science fiction stories. All the series were short-lived. They included *Volume One* (ABC, June 16, 1949 to July 21, 1949), *Escape* (CBS, January 5, 1950 to March 30, 1950), and *Stage 13* (CBS, April 19, 1950 to June 28, 1950).

From the man who created the radio anthology, *Lights Out,* came the provocative drama *Volume One* – a six-part series of psychological thrillers and science fiction tales. Originally the title was *Quiet, Please*! named after Wyllis Cooper's radio series of the same name. *Volume One* premiered on ABC, Thursdays at 9:30 pm. Cooper not only wrote and produced the series but also introduced each episode.

While details about most of the episodes are unavailable, episode number four fell into the category of science fiction. "Number Four" of the series starred Nancy Sheridan as a female senator and James Monks as an astronomer in a strange tale about relationships. The senator whose first name is Ruth and the astronomer whose name is Reed were previously married. Under the pretense of touring the astronomical observatory, 8000 feet above the ground, Ruth admits that she misses her ex-husband and wants him to return with her to Washington D.C. The senator, in a position of power in Washington, makes it clear that if he doesn't return, he will lose his current job. He refuses to leave.

Reed rotates the observatory dome and turns off the lights to highlight a nebula that is seventy light years away. He encourages Ruth to go out on the catwalk to have a better view of the stars. She wants him to turn off the telescope now that she realizes how insignificant earth is compared to the rest of the universe. Reed says he cannot be taken away from his job because he has "friends" in the cosmos. Reed goes on to announce that he has a new love – a jealous one. Ruth replies saying that Reed is a "fool" and that she will ruin him. A woman's large face appears on the observatory's deck. Ruth screams. Reed disappears leaving behind only his scarf.

Escape presented "The Diamond Lens," broadcast on January 19, 1950, which was based on a science fiction story by nineteenth-century writer, Fitz-James O'Brien. The original story focused on a young man who is obsessed with microscopes and the exploration of the tiny world that they reveal. The story later served as the basis for a March 14, 1952 episode of *Tales of Tomorrow*.

Cooper also created a series for CBS titled *Stage 13* which included science fiction stories like a May 10, 1950 entry called "Never Murder Your Grandfather." Two young men played by Leslie Nielsen and Robert Gallagher invent a time machine. Traveling backward in time, one of the men decides to eradicate the other by killing his grandfather before the grandfather has any children. His motive for the killing is to make the time machine all his own.

"Permission to Kill" (May 17, 1950) on *Stage 13* focused on a future society which permits each of its citizens to receive a license to murder one person a year. In 1994, a mutually distrustful couple, played by Alice Reinhart and Daniel Morgan, have a murder license to kill one person. Guess who each plan to kill? The husband ends up murdering his wife but is put on trial. The reason for the trial is not the murder but the fact that he drowned himself after the homicide. Where the trial took place was never clarified for the viewer.

Finally, the anthology produced by MCA, *Stars Over Hollywood*, presented adaptations of several stories by Nelson Bond. For example, the January 3, 1951 entry for the anthology, "My Nephew Norvell," was adapted by Sidney Field from a Nelson Bond story. Joe Grady, about thirty-five, comes back to his apartment building to learn from his landlady, Mrs. McGill, that his nephew is in his apartment. The problem is that Joe doesn't have a nephew. When he goes to his place, he finds a note reading: "Sorry. I can't wait. Power running low. Must refill stellium cartridge. Will return later."[5]

Joe shows Mrs. McGill that there is no one in his apartment. His landlady insists that, after the nephew arrived, no one left the building.

Subsequently, Joe meets his fiancée, Winifred, in the park. They discuss Joe leaving his employer, General Engineers, to work on his own. Winnie doesn't think that it is a good idea and threatens to call off their engagement.

When Joe returns to his apartment, Mrs. McGill says that his nephew is still there. This time Joe sees Norvell, a young man of about twenty-two. Norvell wonders why his uncle is living in an apartment building instead of one of his mansions. Joe is confused. To make sure that his uncle is really Joe Grady, Norvell goes down a list of events in Joe's life including the fact that Joe married in 1956 in Sandusky, Ohio. Norvell states that he is from the year 2003 and that he is really Joe's great grand-nephew. He goes on to say that he is working on Joe's biography and that his family owes its fame and fortune to Joe. Apparently, in the 1960s, Joe created the Hertzian modifier, a counter-gravitational tube, and the hypatomic motor – all of which made space flight possible.

Joe is perplexed to say the least. Norvell begins diagramming the various inventions that he just described. Joe responds that he is no genius – just a normal mechanical engineer, but with the diagrams that Norvell made, Joe thinks he could start to create the various instruments. He asks his nephew to go back to the future to obtain detailed blueprints of the items to help him build them. Norvell promises to return soon.

The following day at work, Joe tells his secretary Doris that he is going to quit and go out on his own. Later, that day, he returns home and sees a note from Norvell that his nephew is having trouble finding the blueprints. Norvell has left him $12,000 to use until he returns.

Joe informs Winnie about quitting his job which she thinks is a big mistake. He also shows her the money that Norvell left him. Winnie returns his engagement ring. Joe leaves her sitting on the park bench.

The next day, Joe receives a panicked phone call from Doris, telling him to come into the office as soon as possible because he has been charged with theft from the company. When he arrives, he finds a police detective there with his former fiancée. Mr. Squeer, the boss, says that Joe broke into the company the previous night and stole plans selling them to an outside interest in return for the cash he showed Winnie. The detective indicates that the money is counterfeit since the serial numbers on it show that it will not be issued for another decade.

A week later, Joe and Doris are strolling through the park. He has been released from custody since Squeer had located the supposedly stolen plans and since there is no proof that he counterfeited the money. Doris mentions that she and her family are from Sandusky, Ohio and that she and Joe should move there. Her father has a tool shed in the back yard that can be converted into a laboratory for Joe. Joe says he can use the diagrams that Norvell originally made to develop the mechanisms for which he is credited in the future as having invented.

Season One of *Tales of Tomorrow*

"Verdict from Space" – August 3, 1951

Cast: Lon McCallister as Gordon Kent
Writer: Theodore Sturgeon
Director: Leonard Valenta

"Verdict from Space" was the premiere episode of the series set in Morgan County, Maine where Gordon Kent is on trial for murdering Professor Sykes, a scientist. No one believes Kent's story about how the death of the professor came about.

Flashbacks reveal what happened. Sykes came to Kent's workshop to ask him to open a metal door in a cave in order to reveal secrets from the past. Inside the cave is a machine that has recorded every physical disturbance to the earth such as earthquakes, volcanic eruptions, and atomic bomb explosions for the past million years. The professor gives Kent $5000 for his work. Initially, the professor had found the machine when the door was open but now it is closed.

When the two find the cave with the door, Kent opens it by applying heat. Kent discovers that part of the machine inside is a transmitter. As the machine records an atomic bomb test, Kent is able to escape from the cavern, but the professor is injured and dies from a cave in. Flashing forward, the jury finds Kent guilty of murder. He makes an impassioned speech that some beings in space are going to arrive on earth since earthlings have invented the atomic bomb which is seen by the extraterrestrials as a threat to them. As he speaks, overhead there is the sound of thousands of space ships entering earth's atmosphere.

The invention of the atomic bomb and its consequences is a prevalent theme in many episodes of the series as well as in other anthologies at the time.

This episode was based on "The Sky Was Full of Ships" by Theodore Sturgeon published in the June 1947 issue of *Thrilling Wonder Stories.* The TV presentation generally follows the short story with some exceptions. The main character's last name is spelled "Kemp" in the story itself but the introductory blurb for the story reads "Kent" like the TV episode. Kemp or Kent is facing a coroner's jury about the death of Alessandro Sykes who had hired Kent to use his concentrated atomic torch to drill through a metal door covering the entrance to a cave found near Switchpath, Arizona. Sykes is an archeologist who had been exploring for Indian artifacts in the desert when he came across a hidden cave housing a transmitter and a recorder. The last time the transmitter worked was after an atom bomb test on earth. When Kent finally cuts through the door, Sykes finds that the recording tape has been replaced with a new tape. Sykes and Kent have to escape the cave when the machines begin to melt and the cave fills up with lava. Sykes postulates that whoever placed the machines in the cave now know that humans have reached the atomic age and the only way to stop further uses of atomic energy on earth is to kill all humans. The experience of seeing the cave fill up with lava is so traumatizing to Sykes that he dies. The building where the coroner's inquiry is being held catches on fire and "the sky is full of ships."

"Blunder" – August 10, 1951

Cast: Robert Allen as Carl
Anne Loring as Jane
Story: Philip Wylie
Adapter: Charles O'Neill
Director: Leonard Valenta

The second episode of *Tales of Tomorrow*, "Blunder," concerned a scientist in the Arctic, Carl Everson, who plans to set off an experiment – a low controlled nuclear reaction, to create a natural furnace to provide power to all of Scandinavia. His wife, Jane is concerned that the experiment may be more dangerous than her husband is saying because it could cut off all the oxygen on earth.

In London, a scientist believes Mrs. Everson is correct about the danger. Also, a scientist in Princeton, New Jersey shares the same concern. He contacts the president to try to stop the nuclear reaction. Carl Everson has cut off all communication with the outside world so as not to be disturbed. Right before the scheduled time for the experiment, Jane Everson tries to turn on the radio, but her husband stops her. Meanwhile, the scientists from England take a plane to the Arctic hoping to stop Everson. The experiment goes off as scheduled with a large nuclear explosion as the screen fades to black.

The short story, "Blunder: A Story of the End of the World," was published in the January 12, 1946 issue of *Collier's*. The story had several differences from the television play. It is set in late May, early June in 1974 where two scientists – Carl Everson, Chairman of Physics at the Oslo Institute, and Hugh Dunn, Dean of Engineering at Glasgow and a Nobel Laureate, are in the Arctic region near the North Pole. They plan to produce cheap electric power for Scandinavia based on two assumptions: volcanic phenomenon is radioactive and certain types of volcanic rock can produce steam. They intend to disintegrate a bismuth band in a mine in such a way to start a slow hot atomic chain reaction. The process would burn for centuries and, since the mine is near the sea, steam from the volcanic rocks could be harnessed as a cheap power source.

Nevertheless, bismuth fusion is relatively new and, research is still ongoing with many governments around the world keeping the subject a secret. The two scientists have rigged a detonator and cable into a mine shaft. They set off the explosion and go to lunch.

Chandra Lalunal, a physicist in India, reads an article titled, “Inquiries into the Binding Fractions of Bismuth” written by Everson and Dunn. Having studied the subject himself, he identifies a mathematical error made by the two scientists. Lalunal seeks to tell the world about the mistake but cannot get anyone’s attention for a radio broadcast on physics. Another scientist, Jeffrey Stackpole in the United States also sees the error in Everson and Dunn’s equation and seeks to find them to report the error. Likewise, Herbert Evans in Chicago becomes aware of the issue. He knows the President of the United States and wants to fly to Washington to report to the President.

Meanwhile, Everson and Dunn begin to have second thoughts about the chain reaction they set off. However, the process back at the mine has already started a perpetual chain reaction. The Polar icecap melts. The Scandinavia Peninsula cracks open, and the opening runs down through Europe. The entire planet becomes a little sun growing ten times larger than its original size spewing incredible energy into space. The end of the world all happened in less than one nineteenth of a second.

The author of the short story, Philip Wylie, is best known for having co-written the novel *When Worlds Collide.*

"A Child Is Crying" – August 17, 1951

Cast: Robin Morgan as Lily Massner
Peggy Allenby as Mrs. Massner
Shirley Eggleston as WAC Corporal
Bert Lytell as Dr. Hardensteen
Donald McClelland as Congressman Folmer
Cal Thomas as General Gates
Story: John D. MacDonald
Adapter: Alvin Sapinsley
Director: Don Medford

"A Child Is Crying" concerned Lily Massner, a nine-year-old prodigy. Set in 1961 at the U.S. Army Proving Ground Guided Missile Section in New Mexico, doctors are examining Lily to find out the source of her advanced knowledge of nuclear physics. A doctor believes that she is a mutation. A congressman thinks Lily should be held at the facility permanently as a defense resource.

Lily refuses to disclose why she is so smart. She begins using telekinesis to control people and reveals that she can predict the future. Lily says that soon there will be a military attack on America but refuses to provide details.

General Gates, the base commander, orders a doctor to force Lily to provide specifics of the pending attack. Lily infers that the attack will occur sometime soon and that the United States would strike first if it knows the enemy. She remarks that an escalating war will destroy the earth. Furthermore, Lily divulges that she was born in order to prevent the destruction of the planet, that there are twenty other beings like her who will survive the attack, and that they will rebuild the world.

The General wants to inject Lily with a truth serum so that she will reveal more details of the pending attack. She is administered the drug and says that the attack will occur in the subsequent two months and that no one will win. While she will survive, no one else at the base will and that the truth serum will reduce her intelligence to that of a normal nine-year old. She then loses her reasoning powers and begins to act like a typical youngster.

As an adult, Robin Morgan who played Lily served as editor of *Ms. Magazine* and helped found the Woman's Media Center with Gloria Steinem and Jane Fonda.

The MacDonald story was previously adapted for a 1950 installment of the anthology, *Lights Out*.

The original story had one significant difference from the *Tales of Tomorrow* presentation. In John MacDonald's version, the child was a boy – not a girl. The boy named Billy was born in Albuquerque, New Mexico near where nuclear experimentation had occurred. John Folmar meets with a general at the Pentagon claiming that Billy is a national resource. He says that the boy's parents are willing to give Billy up for adoption. Billy is adopted by Folmar and taken to a military base in Texas. Like the female in the television version, Billy reveals that he can predict the future and notes that he can foresee an attack on the United States. Nonetheless, he will not divulge the date because of the effect it will have on the time-rhythm continuum.

After seven weeks at the facility in Texas and after several sleepless nights, Folmar confides to Burton Janks, the Security Control Officer, about Billy's abilities. The two men then report the information to W.W. Gates, the head of the school of research.

Folmar comes up with a plan to drug Billy so that he will tell them when the military attack will take place. The young man reveals that he is not a mutation caused by atomic radiation but is a new species of man able to interpret the results of the use of atomic energy. The boy predicts the attack within forty to forty-two days. As in the *Tales of Tomorrow* installment, Billy predicts that he will survive the attack along with others like him scattered over the world but that Folmar, Janks, and others at the base will not. He also says that the results of the drug given to him will impair his intellect. Recovering from the drugs, Billy begins acting like a typical nine-year old wondering why he is at the military base, saying he wants to go home, and begins to cry.

John D. MacDonald is perhaps better known for his crime novels than for his work in science fiction. He authored several works highlighting the investigations of Travis McGee as well as the novel, *The Executioners* which was filmed twice under the title *Cape Fear*. His most popular work concerning science fiction was *The Girl, the Gold Watch and Everything*.

"The Woman at Land's End" – August 24, 1951

Cast: Hailia Stoddard
William Harrigan
Douglas Watson
Robert P. Lieb
Chris Drake
Walter Davis
Story: Wilbur Daniel Steele
Adapter: Mel Goldberg
Director: Leonard Valenta

This presentation for which the kinescope is evidently lost apparently is based on a short story by Wilbur Daniel Steele. Steele was a popular short story writer in the first half of the twentieth century. Some of his short stories also inspired episodes of the 1950s anthologies, *Suspense* and *Danger*.

The short story, "Land's End," takes place at Burnham Head Village in a plastered tenement by the ocean. A woman who is between twenty-five and forty is being looked after by Mrs. Sparrow. Sparrow informs Mr. Mendal that the sick woman's memory is gone. She doesn't know where the woman came from or if she has any relatives.

Mr. Mendal visits the woman who believes that tonight will be her last night on earth. Mendal had found the woman standing in the middle of the road, drenched by a rain storm. He brings a phonograph into the room to play some records for her. Hearing the "Mad Song" from *Lucia* played on the phonograph sung by Mary Farnoe, the woman claims she is the singer. Mendal does not know how to respond. Finally, he says that his house is honored with her presence.

Farnoe had learned from a hotel maid after she had collapsed at the symphony one night that she had only three weeks to live. She was put on a train to travel to see Dr. Westcountry for treatment. In the middle of the night, she got off the train during a rain storm.

Farnoe reminisces about the loves of her life. The only man she loved was a young hospital intern who told her to keep away from all men because they wanted something from her. She then asks Mendal about visiting the bell she hears at land's end.

Mendal picks her up and carries her out of the house to the bell. Farnoe sees a building with two yellow windows before her. She doesn't really recall what happened after that. However, she finds herself in a kind of bed built into the side of a small room. Mendal is holding her saying that she is at Burnham Head at a life-saving station. He gives her some brandy and says that she has recovered from her illness. Mendal calls Farnoe's manager and informs him that the singer will be able to perform in three weeks. Mendal is really Dr. Westcountry who has been treating her all along.

Wilbur Daniel Steele was an author and playwright known for highly dramatic stories.

"The Last Man on Earth" (aka "Knock") – August 31, 1951

Cast: Cloris Leachman
John McQuade
Lon McCallister
Martin Brandt
Andrew Branhan
Story: Frederic Brown
Adapter: Reginald Lawrence
Director: Franklin J. Schaffner

No kinescope or script seems to exist for this presentation of *Tales of Tomorrow*. A Fredric Brown short story, "Knock," served as the basis for the episode. The short story begins with its own little tale,

"The last man on Earth sat alone in a room. There was a knock on the door. . ."

Walter Phelan had been a professor of anthropology at Nathan University until two days earlier when the institution ceased to exist. Two days ago, within one hour, the human race had been destroyed except for him and one woman. In any event, ever since his wife had died, books were Phelan's main interest – not women. Aliens labeled "Zan" had taken over earth. Each Zan was about four feet tall and looked nothing like anything on the planet. The Zan had collected a variety of species and placed them in a zoo including Professor Phelan. They learned to speak English quickly and provided the professor with many books that he had requested.

The Zan are surprised when they find two of the animal species they placed in the zoo dead. The Zan are not familiar with the concept of "death."

Walter is moved to a more spacious room in the zoo where he is introduced to Grace Evans – the last woman on earth. They discuss how the Zan invaded the planet. The Zan arrived in a large space ship that emitted some type of vibration that destroyed almost all animal life. The only reason Walter and Grace, along with the other species, weren't killed is because they were inside the Zan space ship. Walter surmises that the Zan used a low intensity vibration just to make Grace and him and the other species unconscious without killing them. Their one mistake thus far has been assuming that animals on earth were immortal and never died.

Learning that earth species are not immortal, they have reorganized their zoo to have male and female species live together instead of alone. The professor informs Grace that from his observations of the Zan, he believes that anything that would kill earthlings could kill a Zan. One of the Zan tells Walter that one of their colleagues has passed away. The Zan met together and decided, after another one of their number died, that earth is a planet of death and that they will be departing the planet. Walter asks for them to keep his door open before they leave so he can care for the other species in the zoo.

When the Zan had taken Walter to see one of the species of animals that had died originally, he noted that it was a rattlesnake. Its partner was still alive. The professor told the Zan that the one live snake would also die soon because of the loss of its mate unless it was given affection and petting. The two Zan that passed away were bitten by the one remaining rattler.

After the Zan left the planet in their space ship, Walter tells Grace that they have a whole world to plan including deciding about perpetuating the human race. He asks Grace to think it over as the subject seems to embarrass her. She leaves, but after a while, he hears her footsteps coming back.

The story ends as it had begun: "The last man on Earth sat alone in a room. There was a knock on the door. . ."

"Errand Boy" – September 7, 1951

Cast: Joey Walsh
Lee Grant
Richard Purdy
Neil Harrison
Joshua Shelley
Ward Wilson
Story: William Tenn (Phillip Klass)
Adapter: Mel Goldberg

This episode is another among the *Tales of Tomorrow* series for which no kinescope is available.

The original story, published in *Astounding Science Fiction* in June 1947, relayed the tale of Malcolm Blyn and a young errand boy employed at his paint supply company. Hennessey, the foreman at the company, has hired a boy named Ernest who wants to study companies run by "robber barons." Hennessey gives him an empty can and instructs Ernest to fill it with green paint with orange polka dots. Ernest returns with the can full. Hennessey then asks the boy to find a left-handed paint brush. But before the boy leaves, he tells Hennessey that he couldn't find green paint with orange polka dots. Instead, he brought back paint with red polka dots. Blyn, standing nearby, sees the money-making possibilities in selling such a paint mixture.

He catches up with Ernest who reveals to Blyn, the company-owner and salesman, that he is from the year 2169 and that he got the paint from the future. He tells Blyn that the paint is hydrofluoric acid that has been triple-blasted. Blyn tries to figure out how he can manufacture such paint. He asks Ernest where his time machine is. Ernest calls the machine a "chrondronos" but says that Blyn wouldn't know how to operate it. Next, Blyn asks if Ernest has any gadget that foretells the future. The kid replies that he has a distringulatrix, but he can't get one. Blyn finds that he could make millions from the gadget but doesn't know how he could turn it into cash.

Ernest takes Blyn to his time machine and tells him about a trendicle – a statistical analyzer that predicts trends. Blyn attempts to interest Ernest in how robber barons operate so that the kid can witness such machinations after returning to the future to get a trendicle. Blyn wants to obtain one so that he could use it to make money.

Ernest brings back the device, but Blyn thinks it is too difficult to use. He wants a simpler device that he can use to read the financial news in newspapers without entering the data. Ernest goes back again to the future to retrieve an "open" trendicle. A little old lady returns with Ernest this time. She is his teacher. She demands that he return to the future with her and bring back all the items he has shown Blyn. Blyn threatens to hurt the boy unless the woman fetches an "open" trendicle. She returns with the device but then incapacitates Blyn, takes Ernest, the device, and the paint can and goes back to 2169.

Blyn recalls the boy mentioning a Mr. Wenceslaus creating a spirrillix in the present year. Thinking he may use it to earn millions, he goes around the country finding men with a similar last name. He finds one who says he has created a better mousetrap.

For the television episode, instead of applying paint with orange polka dots, the script writer changed the type of paint to one with stripes. A trick camera effect was used to show the boy from the future applying the striped paint to the floor. The paint was put down before the show aired live. A fast switching of cameras hid this advance preparation from viewers.[6]

Philip Klass under the pseudonym William Tenn wrote several science fiction short stories. He was also a professor of English at Penn State University.

"The Monsters" – September 14, 1951

Cast: Paul Langton
Bert Kalmar Jr.
Barbara Boulton
Edward Binns
Peggy Allenby
John McGovern
Richard Shankland
Gene Leonard
Story: Robert Foshko
Adapter: Charles O'Neil

Two young scientists, Marlo and Ro, from Mars make the first trip to earth defying their government's prohibition against such travel. They land in Texas where they are murdered by people who believe they are monsters.

Commenting on this installment, producer George Foley indicated that:

> The point of that show was to make people from Mars look like people from Earth. We try to stay away from the Buck Rogers type of thing. Clothes for the Martians had to be different from ours, of course, but not too strange. So we asked fashion designers what styles might look like twenty-five years from now and created costumes from their designs. They were functional but not much different from now.[7]

For this episode, the Martians appeared to be giants, in relation to earthlings. This was accomplished by scaling sets to one-half normal size, which forced the actors to stoop in coming through doorways. Special camera angles also were used to suggest the larger size of Marlo and Ro to viewers.

"The Dark Angel" – September 28, 1951

Cast: Sidney Blackmer as Tim Hathaway
Meg Mundy as Joanne Hathaway
Don Briggs
Melville Ruick
Story: Lewis Padgett (Henry Kuttner)
Adapter: Alvin Sapinsley
Director: Charles Padgett

A police detective stops by Tim Hathaway's house at night to question him about Tim's wife Joanne. Hathaway reveals that he shot his wife at a night club this evening. He says that he killed her before she killed him. Hathaway then tells the detective the complete story about his wife.

One evening, the Hathaway's family doctor comes by their home and explains to Tim that his wife's rib fracture has healed in a record two days. The doctor also says that Joanne's heart is reducing in size and that she has no appendix. Joanne informs her husband that not only is her body changing but also her mind. She says that she can control objects through mental telepathy. She thinks she is evolving into a higher species and wants to separate from Tim. The next morning, she leaves.

A year later, Tim Hathaway sees her photo in the newspaper about inventing an electronic radiation process at a lab in California. He flies to the lab, meets his estranged wife, but then she physically disappears through the wall of a broom closet.

Four years pass. Hathaway sees her again at a nightclub. She says that she is waiting for someone else and wants Tim to go away. She telepathically kills the bartender for listening to her conversation with her husband. Tim pulls out a gun and shoots her.

The detective informs Tim that Joanne is still alive and that she had been waiting for the detective at the nightclub. The detective kills Tim Hathaway with mental telepathy.

The television episode followed, in general terms, the same plot as the original story which was written by Henry Kuttner in 1946. It begins with a young man talking with Tim Hathaway in a bar. Hathaway relates his story about his wife Joanne when she was thirty-five and he was forty. He and Joanne live in an apartment in Manhattan. When returning from a party driving in a snowstorm, their car skids into a ditch. Joanne gets out of the car while her husband jams his foot on the accelerator. The vehicle is thrust out of the ditch back onto the road. Tim thinks, but knows it was not possible, that his wife lifted the car out of the ditch.

Dr. Farleigh, an endocrinologist, talks with Tim a few weeks later, asking that Joanne see him. He thinks that she may have a form of hypothyroidism. On X-rays it appears that her heart is enlarged and her appendix has disappeared.

That night when Tim returns home, he hears a crooning sound come from their bedroom and sees something move across the floor. When he turns the bedroom light on, he sees a doll beside his wife's feet. The movement of the doll that Tim had witnessed was not that of a puppet or an automation. Joanne confesses that she is changing. Her mind works so much better now, and she can control inanimate objects. She is becoming a completely new type of being. At thirty-five, she is finally maturing to her full potential. She believes that when her father was on a research expedition in Mexico investigating a meteoric crater, the radiation from the crater produced a mutation when her mother gave birth.

While she still loves her husband, she doesn't believe that her love will last as she matures further and will eventually see her husband as an inferior being. The following morning Joanne disappears. Despite hiring a detective agency to find her, Tim has no luck. He believes he sees a photo of a woman like Joanne in a news magazine but, when he makes inquiries, he finds that she has disappeared.

After seventeen years, one day in Central Park, he sees a woman that reminds him of Joanne although she is much younger. The woman reads Tim's mind and declares that she has learned to control her power. Joanne had sought to create an artificial mutation that would duplicate her but was unsuccessful. She is very lonely now. Joanne then kills a homeless man passing by because he had heard their conversation and she doesn't want anyone to know about her except for Tim. Tim leaves feeling that nothing can be done to curb her power. He goes home, retrieves a handgun, and goes to the Met where Joanne said that she would be appearing. He tries to shoot her but has second thoughts and doesn't go through with the act. She yells from the stage at him saying that she will return to him, but he doesn't hear her as the crowd comes forward to subdue him.

The man with whom Tim has been relaying his story was at the Met the night of the attempted assassination and tells Tim what Joanne had said. The man is now married to Joanne. He kills Tim with his power and returns to Joanne – the future mother of his children that will one day rule the earth.

Henry Kuttner, who wrote the short story, also crafted the story, "What You Need," used as the basis for the February 8, 1952 presentation of *Tales of Tomorrow*.

"The Crystal Egg" – October 12, 1951

Cast: Thomas Mitchell as Professor Frederick Vaneck
Edgar Stehli as Mr. Cave
Josephine Brown as Mrs. Cave
Sally Gracie as Georgette, the professor's girlfriend
Gage Clarke as Walker
Story: H.G. Wells
Adapter: Mel Goldberg
Director: Charles S. Dubin

A man visits an antique shop to purchase a crystal egg displayed in the window. The shopkeeper, Mr. Cave, tells the customer that the egg is for sale for five pounds. Since the man has only two pounds ten, Mr. Cave says that the man can collect the egg when he pays the additional two pounds ninety. Mr. Cave wants Professor Vaneck, a physicist, to inspect the egg before the customer returns. Cave leaves the crystal egg with the professor. Vaneck sees the egg glow and becomes obsessed with an arid terrain he discerns inside the egg. The professor believes he is seeing Mars within the egg and spies a one-eyed creature inside.

Mr. Cave returns to the professor's house wanting the egg back since the customer is coming for the item. He runs away with the egg despite Vaneck wanting additional time to analyze it. When Vaneck goes to the antique shop to get the egg, Mrs. Cave informs him that her husband has been killed and the egg is missing. The professor wants to find the man who was purchasing the egg since having the crystal egg will prove his findings about Mars. Nonetheless, Vaneck tells his colleagues what he discovered within the egg. They believe that he has lost his mind.

Vaneck then visits Walker, the publisher of a scholarly journal, to ask him to print the professor's article on his discovery. Walker won't publish the article without seeing the egg himself to verify the accuracy of the article.

Vaneck records his story on a phonograph record in order to convince others to find the egg. He is shot before the recording is completed, and the recording is destroyed.

The original story by H.G. Wells focused mainly on shopkeeper, Mr. Cave, proprietor of C. Cave Naturalist and Dealer in Antiquities, whose store held a mass of crystal worked into the shape of an egg and brilliantly polished. Two men, Reverend James Parker and an Oriental Prince of Boso-Kuni, come into the shop to purchase the egg having seen it in the window. Mr. Cave says the egg is for sale for five pounds but then reveals that the egg has already been promised to another man who intends to purchase it. Mrs. Cave appears and begins arguing with her husband about selling the egg. The Oriental proposes to return in two days to buy the egg if its potential purchaser has not bought it by then.

The following day, Mrs. Cave finds that the egg has been removed from the shop window. She locates it behind some books and places it back in the window. While his wife is having her afternoon nap, Mr. Cave again removes the crystal egg from the window. When his wife discovers the egg missing, she searches the shop. Mr. Cave returns to find his wife on her knees behind the counter. He acts surprised when his spouse tells him the egg is missing.

Mr. Cave lied about not knowing where the egg is. He had given it to Jacoby Wace, a student of science, for safekeeping. Mr. Cave tells Wace that he had discovered the egg to be phosphorescent. One time, while viewing the egg, he saw the image of a wide and spacious strange country. He viewed a moving picture with objects moving slowly in an orderly manner. Mr. Wace can see the same image that Cave has seen. A view of reddish cliffs, bird-like creatures, a vast range of buildings, trees, and a wide canal can be discerned through the egg.

Mr. Cave returns to Wace's apartment often to view the images through the crystal egg. Wace chronicles Cave's descriptions of what he is seeing. Mr. Wace finds that the bird-like creatures are human-like beings with broad silverly wings that fly around the valley and into the buildings. He concludes that the crystal egg is related to an identical egg in the strange world and a being from that world can view earth through its crystal. Wace also surmises that he and Mr. Cave are seeing the landscape and inhabitants of Mars through the crystal.

One day, after Mr. Cave took the egg back to his shop, Wace finds that the shop is closed and learns that Mr. Cave has died clutching the egg. Mrs. Cave had sold the egg and other items in the shop to a fellow tradesman who, in turn, had sold the egg to a tall, dark man in grey.

"Test Flight" – October 26, 1951

Cast: Lee J. Cobb as Wayne Crowder
Vinton Hayworth as Davis
Cameron Prud'Homme as Marty
Harry Townes as Wilkins
Story: Nelson Bond
Adapter: Mel Goldberg
Director: Charles S. Dubin

In "Test Flight," Wayne Crowder, the head of a large corporation, wants to be the first man in space. Much to the dismay of his Board of Directors and other executives of his company, Crowder spends hundreds of millions of dollars to build a spacecraft. He finds an engineer to construct an engine powerful enough to launch the craft. But the man insists that he must be on the first test flight.

When the Board of Directors of Crowder's company prohibits any additional funds to be spent on the project, Crowder forges ahead anyway to purchase the fuel necessary for a launch. Finally, the craft is ready to go into space, but the board fires Crowder. He wants the craft to launch immediately with himself and the engineer on board. After a successful launch with the ship in space, Crowder seeks to return to earth, but the engineer informs Crowder that he has programmed the craft to take him to his home planet – Mars.

At the beginning of the live presentation, actor Lee J. Cobb forgot his lines. As agency executive Robert Lewine pointed out: "When the curtain went up, so to speak, and the lights came on, he got the cue to start, and he was by himself, at his desk, and he could not think of the lines. He went blank. We lost the first two pages of the script."[8]

The story on which this episode is based first appeared in the August 1951 issue of *Esquire* magazine under the title, "Vital Factor" by Nelson Bond. The main outlines of the story are the same as the television episode except for Crowder's fight with his Board of Directors. There is no mention of that in the short story. The story points out that Wayne Crowder made his fortune by selling a simple household product needed by everyone at a penny-profit price that crushed all his competition. Crowder offers $100,000 to the person who can build a powerful enough engine for his space craft to lift it off earth's surface. Wilkins, who says he can use electromagnetism to power the engine, is finally chosen by Crowder to proceed with his plans. Crowder tells Wilkins that he wants to be the first to conquer space since it will make him greater, richer, and stronger – the master of more than one world. Wilkins says that he wants to leave earth to go elsewhere, perhaps to Mars to which he has a sentimental attachment.

Four months after beginning work, the space vehicle launches with Crowder and Wilkins on board. Crowder says that he wants to return to earth to build a larger model and forge a new empire on

Mars. Wilkins slips off his outer clothes revealing a gleaming tight-knit gold cloth outlining his non-human physique and says that he is going to Mars – his home planet.

Nelson Bond (1908 – 2006) wrote several short stories and radio and television scripts. In 1998, Mr. Bond was made an Author Emeritus by the Science Fiction and Fantasy Writers of America.

"Search for the Flying Saucer" – November 9, 1951

Cast: Jack Carter as Vic Russo
Olive Deering as Ginny Walker
Maurice Manson as Saucer Man
Vaughn Taylor as Crazy John
Writer: Mel Goldberg
Director: Charles S. Dubin

Vic Russo arrives at a boarding house in Las Palmas, New Mexico to investigate reports of flying saucers. The boarding house is run by a beautiful young lady named Ginny Walker. Crazy John is one of the inhabitants of the house who likes to play chess with himself. Vic claims that he is a reporter for a New York newspaper and wants to interview town residents about UFO's. Nonetheless, none of the residents want to talk with him about saucers. Crazy John shows Vic a piece of metal that he claims came from a flying saucer and says that one exploded nearby and that a Native American and a reporter had been killed.

Vic reveals that he really is a former pilot for the Army Air Corps who lost his position because he witnessed a flying saucer when airborne. He seeks to prove that they really do exist presumably so he can be reinstated in the air corps. He begins falling in love with Ginny and she with him. Nonetheless, not being able to produce any eyewitness accounts of saucers, he is about to leave the town. As he gets ready to depart, Crazy John invites him to go with him to witness an incoming saucer. Ginny contacts her superior about Vic. Vic returns to the boarding house to get some food before he returns to the place where Crazy John believes flying saucers will appear. When Ginny can't stop Vic from going, she tells her superior that there is no way to stop humans from investigating sightings of UFO's. Her superior responds that she, along with him and all the aliens, might as well return to their home planet.

This episode was from an original script by Mel Goldberg and marked the dramatic debut on television of comedian Jack Carter.

"Enemy Unknown" – November 23, 1951

Cast: Walter Abel
Edith Fellows
Lon McCallister
Story: Theodore Sturgeon
Adapter: Mel Goldberg

Nuclear explosions are occurring all over the world: one in the Sahara Desert, another in the Sierra Madre Range, a third on a small Pacific island. The United Nations establishes a bi-lateral committee to determine the origin of the explosions.

Lieutenant Vincent Otis, Jr., whose father is a preeminent nuclear physicist, meets with a general concerning the explosions. Vince Jr. is a member of Army Intelligence. His father, retired now and suffering from a heart condition, declines to assist the government in determining the cause of the explosions. As the explosions get closer to the continental United States, the general wants Vince Jr. to talk his father into joining the investigation.

Vince meets with his dad, Professor Otis, and his mother Ellen. The Professor doesn't believe that the blasts are coming from America's enemy – the Soviet Union. A fourth blast occurs in Alaska. Vince Jr. attempts to enter his father's laboratory but finds it locked.

He and his dad argue about the father's unwillingness to help the government defend against the blasts. That night, Vince overhears his father on the telephone sending a telegram. The next morning, the professor informs his wife that their son has returned to Washington D.C. Professor Otis tells his spouse what Vince Jr. overheard and that he will return to them soon with a visitor. Vince Jr. and the general come to the Professor's home with the general producing several telegrams that the Professor had been sending telling the government to look for the source of the blasts coming from Mars. The general insists that the Soviet Union is behind the blasts.

The Professor diagrams his theory for the general and Vince Jr. by illustrating that Mars is sending radio waves that bounce off the moon and are deflected into bauxite deposits on earth causing explosions.

Later, the general meets with Dr. Willis, a young physicist who had previously worked for Dr. Otis. Dr. Willis doesn't believe Professor Otis' theory. Willis postulates that forces on earth are behind the blasts. Professor Otis phones the general predicting that the next explosion will be in the Rocky Mountains. He is proved to be correct.

The general, Vince Jr., and Dr. Willis go to Professor Otis' home. The Professor tells them that the next explosion will be in Washington D.C. He suggests that humans need to work together to build sonic towers all over the world in order to jam the signals from Mars. He proclaims that either the towers need to be built or else earth will be sacrificed to bickering among countries. A debate about the Professor's proposal is held at the UN.

Vince Jr., still at his parents' home, learns that his father had done research on the possibility of bouncing radio waves off the moon back to earth. The Professor sought to invite humans to work together on defending earth instead of warring with one another. The Professor doubles over with a severe heart attack. He tells his son that his secret is now with the son. Professor Otis dies. The general calls Vince Jr. who tells him that they must continue to build the towers all over the world.

This episode may have been based on a story by Theodore Sturgeon that he published in the October 1940 issue of *Astounding Science Fiction.*

"Unite and Conqueror" told the tale of two brothers – one a colonel in the military, the other a physicist. Colonel Leroy Simmons is on the Board of Strategy that draws up plans for potential wars. His brother, whom Leroy nicknames "Muscles," develops various technologies for use by the military. His latest creation is a "spy-eye" – a self-propelled information interceptor that works like a drone picking up short-range transmissions and has a camera and audio tape.

Scientists on earth have picked up transmissions from outer space. Subsequently, a bomb is dropped over Lake Michigan from a space ship. Russia then shoots down the space craft that breaks completely apart when it falls to earth. Dr. Simmons volunteers to travel to Russia to investigate the pieces of the craft it has recovered. He finds that the craft was made of an unknown metal.

To stop a potential invasion from outer space, the countries on earth begin to work together to thwart an invasion from outer space. Satellites are launched to monitor any incoming missiles, and a space station is being constructed to orbit earth. Three space ships appear ready to enter earth's atmosphere. Bombs begin to fall from the space crafts which are intercepted by the satellites or else burn up in the earth's atmosphere.

Seven months pass. Dr. Simmons enters his secret laboratory and encounters his brother, the colonel. The colonel accuses his brother of conspiring with the aliens from outer space. Dr. Simmons knew where the alien crafts came from and what they are going to do. He says his plan was to create alien invaders to unify the countries on earth. He reveals a message he recorded for the world to hear. In the message he states that the space ships came from earth – not outside the solar system. The doctor created the illusion of space crafts from a field of binding energy and the use of his spy-eyes in a certain configuration. The bombs were real and came from one of the interceptor satellites that had been launched.

Upon leaving his laboratory, an assassin shoots the colonel thinking he is Dr. Simmons. The colonel originally arranged for his brother to be killed. But when the colonel heard his brother explain what he had done and why, the colonel switched coats with his brother and so allowed the hit man to kill him.

Born Edward Hamilton Waldo on February 26, 1918, Theodore Sturgeon specialized in fantasy, horror, and science fiction stories. His 1944 story "Killdozer!" was adapted as a movie for television in 1974. He also wrote scripts for the original *Star Trek* series including "Shore Leave" and "Amok Time."

"Sneak Attack" – December 7, 1951

Cast: Zachary Scott as Ray Clinton
Royal Beal as the General
Theo Goetz as Dr. Kamrass
Barbara Joyce as Dr. Marnoff
John Seymour as the Secretary of Defense
Richard W. Shankland as the President
Peter von Zerneck as the Colonel
Story: Russell V. Ritchey
Adapter: Mel Goldberg
Director: Leslie Gorall

Set in 1960, at a hospital behind the Iron Curtain, Major Ray Clinton is recovering from gunshot wounds to his leg. Clinton is interviewed by a military officer from the Eastern bloc who says Clinton is a spy and crossed into the country illegally.

Clinton learns that his wounds are only superficial and that he can walk. Dr. Marnoff reveals that her country has developed a secret weapon for a sneak attack on America and that the control center for the weapon is in the hospital.

Meanwhile, in the United States, dozens of robot-piloted aircraft land at the airports for America's largest cities. The military has no idea what is inside the planes. They begin drilling into one located in Denver. The plane explodes destroying the city of Denver. The President addresses the nation about the sneak attack. The enemy country wants to take over America or else blow it up.

Clinton learns what is happening. He is told that a Heterodyne bomb is responsible for the blast in Denver. The President has fifty-five minutes to find a way to disable the bombs contained in the foreign aircraft or else the country will be turned over to the enemy. Clinton, with the help of Dr. Marnoff, works to stop the other bombs from detonating. With four minutes to go before all the bombs explode, Clinton disarms the enemy colonel and blows up the control center for the bombs.

A very short story in the June 26, 1948 issue of *Collier's* magazine served as the basis for this episode. The President of the United States receives the following letter from Ambassador Miturski of the Soviet Union:

> For many months our two countries have endeavored, through diplomatic means, to adjust their differences and live at peace in the world. We have accomplished nothing. Our two ideologies cannot live peacefully on the same earth. The inevitable arms race, if we attempt it, can lead only to the destruction of both nations and their allies. We feel that it would be foolhardy to continue our diplomatic bickering when all our problems could be easily solved.

The letter went on to state:

> Therefore, we have taken the following action:

1. Twelve B-29 airplanes, bearing American Army markings but manned by our crews, and each loaded with three atomic bombs, have landed at the following cities: San Francisco, Los Angeles, Seattle, Kansas City, Washington, Pittsburgh, Detroit, New Orleans, Philadelphia, Boston, New York, and Chicago.
2. Immediately upon landing, each airplane was joined by two United States Army trucks. Each truck was loaded with one atomic bomb. These trucks, operated by American citizens sympathetic to our government, were then driven to strategic points within each city.

The letter contained the following demands of the President:

1. Order the immediate disarmament of all American troops and all naval and military installations.
2. Ground all aircraft.
3. Order all naval vessels to put into the nearest port and await our commands.
4. Order all armed forces in occupied territories to lay down their arms and prepare to receive our commanders, who will accept their surrender.
5. Inform your people, by radio, that any resistance will result in catastrophe, and that any exodus from the cities we have named will be cause for action. The populations of these cities will be treated as hostages.
6. Inform your people that our representatives will take over the government of the United States at noon tomorrow. American citizens sympathetic to our government will take over all state and city governments at the same time.
7. Order your people to surrender all privately owned arms to our representatives.

8. Inform your people that our troops and administrators will begin to arrive at noon tomorrow. They will land at Boston, New York, and cities on the West Coast. Their landing will not be resisted.[9]

The letter went on to indicate that the President has two hours to accept or reject these conditions. If the terms are not accepted or if there is no reply, bombs will be exploded first in New York and then in other cities.

The story ends with the President asking his cabinet what shall we do?

The script by Mel Goldberg obviously expanded on the original story significantly and added a more comforting ending. Colonel Russell V. Ritchey, who wrote the original story, was a member of the United States Air Force who founded the Squadron Officers School and was its first commandant.

"The Invader" – December 21, 1951

Cast: William Eythe as Roy
Eva Gabor as Laura
Edgar Stehli as Burroughs
Salem Ludwig as Chandler
Farrell Pelly as McQueen
Writers: Robert Foshko and Mort Zarcoff
Director: Don Medford

On a ship, a scientist and his assistants pull up a cage full of organisms from the sea floor. Burroughs, the scientist, and his assistant Laura analyze the specimens. Burroughs is highly critical of his son and Laura's fiancé Roy, also a scientist who really seeks to be a writer. Chandler, the diver, says that he is no longer going to make any more dives into the ocean. Everyone on board the ship, including Captain McQueen witness what they think is a meteor crashing into the water. Burroughs wants Chandler to dive in to explore what crashed, but the diver refuses. Roy volunteers to dive to explore the crash.

When resurfacing, Roy appears to be possessed by an alien creature but tells his father that he only found a meteor at the bottom of the sea. Roy then strangles McQueen to death. Burroughs instructs the ship to return to San Francisco. Laura notices that Roy doesn't appear to be himself. He reveals his alien countenance and kills Laura and Chandler. He confronts Burroughs saying that Roy is dead inside his spacecraft and that the only issue of importance is science – not the individual. The alien was sent to inspect earth to determine if the planet was suitable for invasion. Burroughs then turns on poisonous gas to kill the alien.

The co-writers of this episode, Robert Foshko and Mort Zarcoff, both became television producers later in their careers. The former produced *The Man from U.N.C.L.E.* and *The Survivors*; the latter produced *It Takes a Thief* and *The Misadventures of Sheriff Lobo.*

"The Dune Roller" – January 4, 1952

Cast: Bruce Cabot as Sam Thorne
Truman Smith as Cap Zanse
Nancy Coleman as Jean Burges
Nelson Olmstead as Dr. Carl Burges
Lee Graham as Sally
Story: Julian C. May
Adapter: Charles O'Neil
Director: Don Medford

The story opens with Cap Zanse telling Sally about the dune roller – a legend around Lightning Island in Lake Michigan. It is a large rock that expands and moves. Sally's father, Sam Thorne, is a biologist exploring the island. He is working with Dr. Carl Burges and his wife Jean. Sam contends that specimens he had picked up have grown together and expanded in size. Dr. Burges believes that the specimens are from a meteor that crashed into the island several years ago and that the meteor may be trying to put itself back together.

Later, the scientists discover that the specimen has grown larger and rolled outside their cabin. Cap has some additional samples of the specimen at his cabin nearer the water. While in his abode, Cap sees a light on the lake. He flees his cabin to return to Sam's place, but the light follows killing him. The scientists begin to believe in the story of the dune roller which is like a giant rolling flame thrower. Jean goes to Cap's cabin and sees the light again. Meanwhile, Dr. Burges plans to neutralize the dune roller by blowing it up. Sam takes dynamite and a detonator to destroy the dune roller using small pieces of the rock as bait. He blows it into a thousand pieces with the rocks beginning to fuse back together.

A story in *Astounding Science Fiction* (December 1951) by J.C. May was the inspiration for this episode. "Dune Roller" was Ms. May's first professional work as a writer. The television episode followed the same general outline as that published in the science fiction magazine but with several differences in the characters.

Dr. Ian Throne, a widower, is an ecologist investigating plants on an island in Lake Michigan. He discovers small drop-like amber objects shaped like a marble but with a tail. His friend Kirk MacInnes communicates with Throne via a ham radio. One day, while delivering the doctor's mail, he brings with him in his forty-foot boat his niece, Jeanne Wright.

Later, a little boy brings a badly injured toad to Dr. Throne. It swallowed some tiny amber stones that ruptured its digestive track. The doctor takes the stones and mails them to Willy Seppel, another friend of his, for analysis.

Meanwhile, a tramp, Gimpy Zandbergen, walking near Lake Michigan, while a thunderstorm strikes the island, dies. Dr. Throne finds his body which has been burned black on one side. The medical examiner concludes that the man had died after being struck by lightning. But Thorne had found a fist-sized amber under Zandbergen's body.

Seppel analyzes the specimens he received from Thorne and discovers that they generate heat. The following day, Dr. Thorne discovers that the fist-sized specimen he found is gone. The drawer in which he had placed it has a hole in the bottom. There is also a hole in the outside door. Thorne follows a track made by the specimen in the sand leading to the lake.

Out in her uncle's boat, Jeanne Wright comes upon a glowing globe bearing down on the water craft. She attempts to contact her uncle and Throne via the radio in the craft. She succeeds in contacting Thorne and tells him that the globe is chasing the boat. He instructs her to throw the amber stone he had previously given her overboard. The Coast Guard finds the cruiser drifting and out of gas. In shock, Jeanne is admitted to the hospital.

Thorne decides to do an experiment with seven amber drops he has. Placing them in a circle on a sand dune, the largest drop begins to move down the dune. One of the smaller drops follows it. Thorne prevents the other drops from rolling away. The large globe that had chased Jeanne in the boat appears rolling up the dune to where Thorne is. With great effort, the doctor is able to escape the globe and detonate explosives he had planted in the sand to destroy the glowing orb.

The story ends: "High on a dune above the lake, smoke still rose faintly from a blackened crater in the sand. Two of the grains of sand, which gleamed in the moonlight a bit more golden than the rest, tumbled down together into a sheltered hollow to begin anew the work of three hundred years." [10]

"Frankenstein" – January 18, 1952

Cast: John Newland as Victor Frankenstein
Lon Chaney Jr. as the Monster

Mary Alice Moore
Farrell Pelly
Peggy Allenby
Raymond Bramley
Michael Mann
Story: Mary Shelley
Adapter: Henry Myers
Director: Don Medford

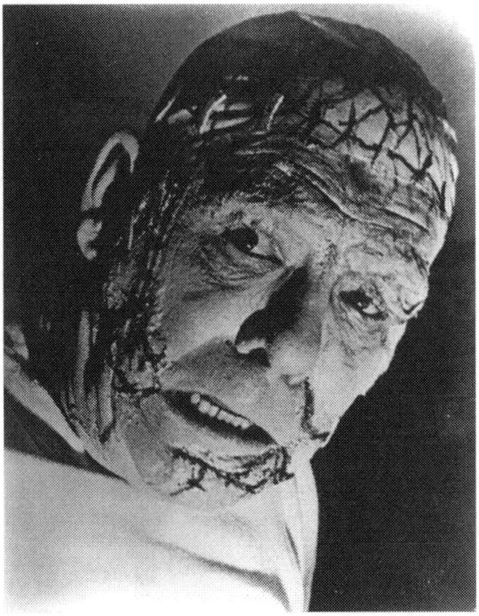

Lon Chaney Jr. as the Monster in *Tales of Tomorrow*. Chaney appeared in several classic horror movies in the 1940s such as *The Wolf Man*, *Son of Dracula*, and *The Ghost of Frankenstein*. He continued his film career in the 1950s, 60s, and 70s as well as guest starring on a number of television series.

This adaptation of the Mary Shelley novel, set in the twentieth century, featured Dr. Frankenstein who seeks to create the perfect man. In his remote laboratory, Dr. Frankenstein animates his creature who then escapes the laboratory terrorizing the doctor's domestic staff and his son. The creature becomes outraged after seeing his face in the mirror. After the monster kills Dr. Frankenstein's maid, the doctor pledges to destroy it. Frankenstein shoots the creature as it jumps out of a window in the laboratory into a lake below. Nevertheless, the monster returns. The doctor lures the creature back into his laboratory where it is electrocuted and finally dies.

This episode marked *Tales of Tomorrow* becoming a weekly series on ABC instead of airing only every other week.

When Lon Chaney as the monster was supposed to break prop chairs, the actor gently sets the chair down and says "Break! Break!" waving his arms around. According to ad agency executive Robert Lewine, who was viewing the live performance at the time, Chaney was inebriated during the presentation. The actor apparently thought it was a dress rehearsal instead of the actual televised show. "He had (already) done a dress rehearsal, and gone into his dressing room, and drank and drank, and when he came back, he didn't know what was going on. He goofed about three or four lines of dialogue. Our director Don Medford was so upset that he wanted to hit Lon! Except Lon was too big for him."[11]

"20,000 Leagues under the Sea"- January 25, 1952 and February 1, 1952

Cast: Thomas Mitchell as Captain Nemo
Leslie Nielsen as Farragut
Brian Keith as Peters
Bethel Leslie as the Girl
John S. Hamilton as Swede
Eddie Hyans as Slay
Roger Dekoven as the narrator, Jules Vern
Story: Jules Vern
Adapters: Max Ehrlich, Harry Ingram, and Gail Ingram
Director: Don Medford

The story by Jules Vern dealt with an expedition put together by the United States government to find a mysterious sea monster that had been sighted by sailors from several countries. French marine biologist Pierre Aronnax and his servant join the expedition along with Canadian whaler Ned Land. After a lengthy search, their frigate called the Abraham Lincoln, locates the monster which turns out to be a submarine, the Nautilus, constructed and commanded by Captain Nemo. Aronnax, Land, and Conseil, Aronnax's servant, are rescued by Captain Nemo after being thrown into the sea when the Nautilus damages the Abraham Lincoln. Aronnax, Conseil, and Land visit many regions of the open seas. One day, Ned Land sees a chance to escape the Nautilus when he spies land. He, along with Aronnax and Conseil, find refuge on an island off the coast of Norway as the Nautilus is caught in a deadly whirlpool.

The initial episode of the *Tales of Tomorrow* two-part adaptation, "The Chase," has Captain Nemo sinking Farragut's ship and taking the commander along with Peters, Farragut's assistant, captive. Farragut, who piloted the Naval frigate Abraham Lincoln, had been ordered to sweep the oceans for an underwater monster preying on shipping.

Nemo had taken to the sea because his wife had left him for another man. He believes the sea is a pristine paradise, while only evil men inhabit the land. Nemo's Nautilus roams the seven seas finding and sinking ships.

In part two, "The Escape," Farragut plots to escape the Nautilus. Nemo's daughter falls in love with him. When Nemo catches the commander kissing his daughter, he puts Farragut and Peters in chains. Farragut devises a plan to escape the Nautilus with Peters and Nemo's daughter. The daughter convinces her father to allow Farragut, Peters, and her to leave the Nautilus. The captain then vows that his vessel will no longer terrorize the seas since his daughter may be on a ship that he would otherwise destroy.

In reviewing the TV adaptation, Jack Gould of *The New York Times* wrote:

As presented on two consecutive Friday evenings on "Tales of Tomorrow" over the American Broadcasting Company network, the saga of Captain Nemo and The Nautilus resembled nothing so much as a soap opera staged in an aquarium.

Incredible as it may seem, the classic in prophecy turned into a "boy-meets-girl" story with the redoubtable captain as just a mean old daddy who stood in the way of young romance.

In order to get the Verne work into an hour's running time, it goes without saying that the staff of "Tales of Tomorrow" would have to take considerable license with the original. But this hardly seems reason for the producer, George Foley Jr., and the writers, Harry and Gail Ingram, to distort the whole basic theme and undertake a submarine version of "Sailor Beware!"[12]

"What You Need" – February 8, 1952

Cast: William Redfield as Tom Carmichael
Edgar Stehli as Peter Talley
Story: Henry Kuttner (Lewis Padgett)
Adapter: Mel Goldberg
Director: Charles S. Dubin

Tom Carmichael, a struggling writer and journalist, enters a shop, Peter Talley's Curios, whose slogan is "I Have What You Need." Carmichael asks Talley what he needs. The shopkeeper gives Carmichael a bag containing a large pair of scissors and tells the writer to keep the scissors on his person. Carmichael wants to investigate how Talley determines what people want and why he charges some customers exorbitant amounts for the wares he gives them. Talking to a news editor about the proposed article, Tom gets his scarf caught in a machine and uses the scissors to cut the scarf preventing him from strangling to death.

Carmichael returns to the shop to thank Talley for saving his life. He wants the shopkeeper to tell him about his future. Talley says that he has a machine that predicts possible future occurrences but refuses to explain to the writer what possibilities the future holds for him. Carmichael persists and threatens to publicize Talley's predicting machine. For his silence, Talley says that he will give Carmichael what he needs. While using his machine, Talley sees that in the future he will be shot to death.

Carmichael informs his girlfriend that he is going to steal Talley's machine. By messenger, he receives a pair of shoes from Talley. Putting them on, he slips on the icy pavement in front of an oncoming car which kills him.

Talley informs his wife what he did. He explains he saw that he would have been murdered by Carmichael when the writer attempted to steal the machine. Talley then destroys the predicting machine.

Rod Serling adapted the same story for an episode of *The Twilight Zone*. In his adaptation, an itinerant peddler, not a shop owner with a predicting machine, enters a bar asking patrons what they need. One man, a conman named Fred Renard, at the bar approaches the peddler and asks him what he needs. The old man gives him a pair of scissors. Later, while going up in an elevator, Renard's scarf is caught in the elevator door. He uses the scissors to cut his scarf so he doesn't strangle. Renard finds the peddler again and receives a leaky fountain pen which drops ink on the name of a racing horse in the newspaper. He bets on the horse and wins. Renard returns to the salesman and demands something else. The man says that Renard needs something that he can't give him like serenity and a sense of humor. Renard takes a pair of shoes from the peddler, puts them on, and suffers the same fate as Carmichael did in the *Tales of Tomorrow* episode.

The actual short story, first published in the October 1945 *Astounding Science Fiction*, was closer to the *Tales of Tomorrow* version than *The Twilight Zone* episode.

Tim Carmichael, who works for a trade paper that specializes in economics, sees a sign, "We Have What You Need" in a shop window. His curiosity piqued, he walks in. The shop keeper, Peter Talley, asks if he can help him. When Carmichael says that he may want to do a story about the shop, Talley responds that he is not sure if he would want the publicity.

Carmichael observes Talley selling an egg to a customer for $5000. After trying unsuccessfully to find out precisely what type of store Talley runs, Carmichael leaves. He returns later that afternoon. He says that he has been following customers of the store to determine what they have been buying. Carmichael observed that the shop's customers really do not know what they're purchasing until they unwrap their little bundles.

Talley says that he runs a credit business. Customers generally don't pay him right away. They wait to determine if the product proves satisfactory to them. Carmichael says that he wants to be a customer of the store. Talley goes to a back room, puts his eye to a binocular plate, and moves a calibrated dial. He instructs his errand boy what to find for Carmichael. He tells Carmichael that he will sell him what he needs for $5. He doesn't want paid right away. Only if Carmichael is satisfied with what he gives him does he want to be reimbursed. Also, if Carmichael is satisfied, Talley doesn't want him to come back to the shop and never mention it to anyone. He then gives the reporter a neatly-wrapped package. When Carmichael unwraps the parcel, he finds a pair of shears.

After Carmichael returns to the office to check on a story he had written, his scarf becomes caught in the Linotype machine. He retrieves the shears and cuts the scarf so he isn't strangled to death.

The next morning, Carmichael returns to Talley's shop and gives him $5. Talley says that he saw what was going to happen to

Carmichael with his machine which predicts the future and that is how he knows what people will need. He insures life, health, and happiness. Carmichael tells him that he wants to be a permanent customer at Talley's shop. Talley's machine predicts that Carmichael will next need a pair of plastic-soled shoes for $500.

Talley, through his machine, sees ten years into the future. Carmichael now wants to control the machine for himself. He returns to the shop with a gun and shoots Talley in the head. This was not the first time that the machine showed Talley his own lifeless body. Viewing through the machine again, Talley sees Carmichael wearing the plastic-soled shoes as he slips off a subway platform into an oncoming train. Tim Carmichael of today had to atone for the Carmichael of ten years in the future.

Among other science fiction stories, Henry Kuttner (1915-1958) contributed to a planned television series, *Tales of Frankenstein*, to be produced by Hammer Films and Columbia Pictures. The unsold pilot was made in 1958.

Kuttner and his wife Catherine were credited with writing the teleplay for the pilot. Starring Anton Diffring as Baron Von Frankenstein, the Baron's creature attacks him because his brain came from a murderer. The Baron wants to replace the brain with one from a good man. Max and Christine Halpert (Richard Bull and Helen Westcott) go to the Baron's castle because Max is suffering from a serious malady and Christine believes that the Baron can treat her spouse. Saying he can't help her husband, the Baron asks the couple to leave.

They return to the inn where they are staying with Max close to death. Max passes away and is buried. After everyone leaves the graveside funeral, the Baron bribes the grave keeper and takes Max's brain to transplant in his creature.

The following morning, Christine returns to her husband's grave and finds a locket that she had placed around his neck near the grave. She speaks with the grave keeper about why her husband's grave wasn't properly closed. He reveals that the Baron told him to leave the grave open.

Christine goes to see the Baron. He keeps her from entering his castle because his creature is making noise, but she enters anyway. The Baron now addresses the creature as Max, but the creature doesn't obey the Baron's commands. The creature goes after Christine picking her up. When he sees himself in a mirror, he reacts in horror to his appearance. The Baron shoots the creature, but the bullet doesn't stop him. The monster goes after the Baron. Christine tells the creature that the Baron did what she asked him to do. The creature falls in a pit. Christine asks the Baron to leave him there. The Baron is subsequently arrested for grave robbing.

"Age of Peril" – February 15, 1952

Cast: Phyllis Kirk
Dennis Harrison (aka Dennis Patrick) as Larry Calhoun
Don Briggs as Mr. Rand
John McGovern as Dr. Chapell
Maurice Burke
Skedge Miller
Phil Minoff
Story: Frederic Brown
Adapter: Andrew J. Russell
Director: Don Medford

"Crisis, 1999" by Fredric Brown was the basis for this installment titled "Age of Peril." Set in 1965, Larry Calhoun is a government agent investigating the theft of portions of plans for a top-secret guided missile from a factory scheduled to manufacture certain parts. He wants to use a special lie detector that, if one passes the test, can mean the person will never be prosecuted for the crime of which they are suspected. Calhoun gives the test to virtually all employees of the factory except for the facility's security officer, Mr. Rand, who refuses to take the test. While calling for a court order, Calhoun detects a tap on a telephone line. He then sets up a fake call saying that new plans for the missile have arrived hoping that the real culprit will take the bait.

Late that night, George Ellwood breaks into the office to steal the most recent plans. Ellwood claims innocence and volunteers to take the lie detector test. He passes it showing his innocence.

Calhoun investigates how Ellwood beat the test and learns that several other suspected criminals in the country have done the same. Calhoun finds that Dr. Chapell, who had helped invent the lie detector, has divulged that he and his colleagues have been working with subjects across the country to fool the lie detector. He demonstrates what he has been doing. Chapell hypnotizes suspects into denying any crime they committed. After the hypnosis, the subjects do not recall what they did. The doctor says that his treatment cures criminals of their deviant behavior and they can never commit crime again. Calhoun phones his chief to allow the doctor's treatments to continue.

The short story on which this presentation was based was first published in the August 1949 issue of *Ellery Queen's Mystery Magazine* as a "futuristic detective story." The story focused on Bela Joad, the greatest detective in the world and, also, evidently a master of disguise. Joad returns from Europe and reads in the newspapers, about the kidnapping of Dr. Ernst Chappel, a criminology professor at Columbia University. He also reads a story about the acquittal of Paul Girard for murdering his rival for control of North Chicago gambling.

Joad goes to meet Chief Dyer Rand who informs Joad that out of every ten crimes committed in Chicago, seven are unsolved because, in most cases, the police know who is guilty but can't prove it.

The underworld is beating lie detector tests. The Chief wishes that lie detector tests had never been legalized. Rand knows that

Paul Girard killed his rival. He took the case to court even though he was aware that he would lose. He did that in order to have Joad return to the United States to meet with him. The Chief wants Joad to find out how underworld criminals are beating the lie detector tests.

Joad requests a list of the criminals who have beaten the test. He tells the Chief that he is going to stage a murder and then have the Chief question the murderer. Joad plans to be the murder victim. He registers under the name of Martin Blue at a cheap hotel in the heart of Chicago's underworld. Joe Zatelli, a restaurant owner, thinks he murdered Blue for rifling his cash register. However, Blue was shot with blanks. Joad then tells Chief Rand who shot him. The police pick up Zatelli. He undergoes a lie detector test which he passes while denying he had killed Blue. The police also ask Zatelli what other crimes he may have committed but, according to the lie detector test, he hadn't committed any of them. Joad seeks to find out how the test is being beaten.

Joad devises another plan. He asks the police to tail Zatelli and Paul Girard as well as others who have beaten the test. He tells Rand that he is looking for Dr. Ernst Chappel who disappeared two years earlier.

Joad becomes a legend in the Chicago underworld using the name Willie Ecks. The police arrest him for the murder of his worst enemy. An acquaintance of Ecks comes to his hideout and tells him that for $10,000 he can solve his problem of being arrested for the supposed murder. He can put Ecks in touch with a man who can show him how to beat a lie detector test.

Late that evening, a man knocks on Willie's door. The man is Dr. Chappel. Early in the morning, Joad goes to Rand's apartment and tells the Chief that this is his last case as a private detective. His next career will be teaching crooks to pass lie detector tests. Chappel has been getting crooks to confess their crimes to him and then hypnotizing them telling the crooks they are not criminals and never have been. When the police then give them a lie detector test, they, as a result of the hypnosis, believe they are innocent. Joad tells the Chief that the men undergoing hypnosis hardly ever commit a subsequent crime. Joad seeks to partner with Chappel to spread the hypnotherapy to other cities to, in the long run, reduce crime.

Frederic Brown, a science fiction, fantasy, and mystery writer, published his first science fiction story, "Not Yet the End," in 1941. He may be best known for his short story, "Arena," which was the basis of the January 19, 1967 episode of *Star Trek*.

"Memento" – February 22, 1952

Cast: Boris Karloff
Barbara Joyce
Writer: Samuel Elkin

A physicist has spent his career constructing a spacecraft that can travel to Mars. Subsequently, he finds that he cannot make the trip because of ill health. Embittered, he seeks to destroy his creation until fate alters his plans.

The Internet Movie Database attributes the story for this episode to Thomas Thompson, a writer of tales about the Old West. Thompson did publish a short story titled "Memento" in the November, 1951 issue of *Zane Grey's Western Magazine*. However, it had nothing to do with science fiction and a planned trip to Mars. Rather the story dealt with Jim Willie, an Apache, who had been raised by a Quaker family who owns a cattle ranch. Brad Eccles, Jim's adoptive father, is engaged in a dispute with a neighboring rancher, Cort Bailey, over water rights for Bailey's cattle. Eccles plans to fence in the spring on his property that Bailey wants to use to water his cattle. Jim Willie shoots Bailey as Bailey is about to shoot Eccles in the back. Willie then leaves his adoptive family and goes back to the Apache tribe.

From the sparse details about the television episode, it seems that the story line is somewhat like the Robert Heinlein short story "Requiem." In that story, D.D. Harriman, a wealthy businessman, has always dreamed of traveling to the moon. His partners prevented him from taking early flights to the moon for fear that an accident would occur and end the company's business in space flight. Now, since space flight is commonplace, Harriman is too old to pass the medical exam for space travel. Not wanting to give up his dream of going to the moon, Harriman bribes two spacemen to take him there. He finally lands on the moon only to die shortly thereafter.

Perhaps writer Samuel Elkin adapted the Heinlein story for *Tales of Tomorrow* and changed the lead character from a business tycoon to a physicist and the place of destination from the moon to Mars. Another possibility is that this episode was based on an original script by Samuel Elkin. Elkin scripted many episodes of anthologies in the 1950s including *Kraft Theatre*, *Danger*, and *Inner Sanctum*.

"The Children's Room" – February 29, 1952

Cast: Claire Luce as Rose
Terry Greene as Walt
John Boruff as Bill
Una O'Connor as Edythe
Lisa Ayers as Miss Perkins
Charles Kenney as the man in the Cloakroom
Grant Roberts as the First Child
Mark Henderson as the Second Child
Nancy Ann Kramer as the Third Child
Story: Raymond F. Jones
Adapter: Mel Goldberg
Director: Don Medford

"The Children's Room" is about a mother named Rose and father Bill whose son Walt is a child prodigy. Walt reads mysterious books from the Children's Room at the local university's library. The library says they do not have a Children's Room, but Bill Davis finds such a room behind a blank wall in the building. Bill reads a book about human mutations that are superior to the average human. Both Mr. Davis and his son are mutants. He is told that his son will be taken from his wife and him. Only mutants can see the Children's Room.

Subsequently, Bill Davis learns that his mutation is slight and of no use to the mutants but that Walt will come when he is ready. His parents talk with Walt who confesses that he doesn't want to go away. His father rips up the book Walt has been reading and suggests taking Walt and his mother away from their home on a vacation to Maine.

Walt finds another mysterious book in his room which instructs him to leave home. He goes to the library after leaving a note for his parents.

The story that inspired the episode contains many more details about the interactions between Rose, Bill, and Walt that couldn't be included in a thirty-minute TV episode. The father, Bill Starbrook, is the Chief Engineer for Bradford Electronics. His son Walt has an I.Q. of 240 and borrows strange books from the local university's library. Bill reads some of the books that relate a fairy-tale-like story about a group of men with different mental and physical attributes. The book was magically distributed all over earth and led the men with special attributes to find one another.

The following morning, Walt, who is suffering from a cold and must stay home, asks his dad to return the book to the Children's Room in the university library. Bill goes to the library where the librarian says there is no children's department in the facility. On his way out of the building, Bill sees a sign above a door that reads, "Children's Room." The librarian in the room, Miss Edythe, requests that Bill review other books in the series that his son is reading to offer his critique. Walt is delighted to get more books and wants his dad to read them to him. The new books further describe the story of the "different" men. Since his father can understand the book, Walt assumes that his dad is one of the "different" men. Bill realizes that both he and his son are mutants. The book's stated purpose is to accelerate the evolutionary rate of the human race by salvaging the beneficial mutations which have been wasted through the years. Bill goes to see his neighbor, Professor Martin, who is the head of the ancient language department at the university, but Martin finds the words in the book unintelligible.

Bill returns to the Children's Room the next day to see Miss Edythe. She tells him that only one other adult in the past 500 years has been suitable material for the colony of mutants. Miss Edythe also explains that the group has been working to maintain the superiority of the human race in the face of an evolutionary lag from which it suffers. By proper utilization of the mutants, humans will evolve to outstrip competitive species in the galaxy who threaten human existence. In addition to understanding the special language in the books that mutants can understand, only mutants can enter the Children's Room which is invisible to regular people. She invites Bill to join with the other mutants and sever ties with his wife and friends. However, Bill wants to be tested to determine what uses his mutant traits will be in the new society before deciding to join it.

A Dr. Rogers exams Bill but finds no mutations that he can contribute to the advancement of man's evolution. Bill only has mutations that allow him to understand the special language in the books and see the Children's Room. Nonetheless, his son, Walt, has three special mutations that the group seeks. Dr. Rogers advises Bill to follow the teachings provided to Walt so he can learn the details of the crisis that faces humanity. If he doesn't, the Council will forcibly take Walt, but the Council will replace him with an identical substitute – a replica of the person taken, often without the family's knowledge.

Bill leaves and, in the quiet of his office at work, he realizes that there may be no alternative to letting Walt go and accepting his substitute.

At home, Bill informs his wife of what he has learned about Walt. Rose doesn't believe the story he tells her. He resigns himself to the fact that his wife can't comprehend what will happen to their son. Bill begins to read future volumes of the books for Walt. The technical information in the books, Bill believes, is useful to present society, and he has photostats made of the pages but they turn out to be unintelligible. Bill decides to read the pages and record his readings.

In the meantime, Walt has been teaching his mother how to read the books. She begins to understand them and realize what will happen to her son. The following day, Walt is told that he will be leaving his family. Some emergency has arisen. The Children's Room is to be moved to another time right away because an important mutation is about to be destroyed in some future time.

Bill drives Rose and his son to the library. Walt walks into the Children's Room, and the room disappears. Rose and Bill start back to their car and see a figure in the back seat – Walt's homolog, his substitute.

Raymond F. Jones, whose 1947 short story published in *Fantastic Adventures*, served as the basis for the *Tales of Tomorrow* episode, is probably most famous for writing the novel, *This Island Earth.*

"Bound Together" – March 7, 1952

Cast: Nina Foch
Robert Webber
Russell Hardie
Leola Harlowe
Dario Barrie
Writer: Mel Goldberg
Director: Unknown

An astronaut who has been reported missing on a trip to the Red Planet unexpectedly returns to his fiancée after being gone for a long period of time. In the meantime, she has fallen in love with someone else. The story takes place in the offices of a government agency in Washington D.C. where rockets are dispatched to outer space.

After *Tales of Tomorrow*, Mel Goldberg wrote for a wide variety of television series ranging from *Mr. Novak* to *The Big Valley.* He also co-scripted the 1968 Clint Eastwood movie *Hang 'Em High.*

"The Diamond Lens" - March 14, 1952

Cast: Franchot Tone as Andre Lapalne
Luis Van Rooten
Rudolf Justice Watson
Theo Gietz
Nina Varela
Robert Bernard
Harold B. Clememko
Story: Fitz James O'Brien
Adapter: Max Ehrlich
Director: Don Medford

Set in Paris, Andre Lapalne, who is about to face the guillotine, confesses to a priest about a diamond microscope lens he developed – a perfect lens that can reveal everything placed under it.

Flashbacks relate how Lapalne's current situation came about. Andre entertains a new tenant, Gaston Dubois, in his apartment building who works in a jewelry store. Gaston describes a 150-carat diamond in the store. Gaston refuses Andre's demand to break into the shop to steal the diamond, and so Andre steals the diamond himself. When Gaston tries to convince Andre to return the diamond, Andre murders him.

Andre uses a special liquid acid to shape the diamond into a lens. The police come by to question Andre about the death of Gaston. Andre reveals that he knows the incident involved a stolen diamond which was not published in the papers. After the policeman departs, Andre uses the lens for the first time and sees incredible detail in a drop of water. He reports his work to the French Academy while his landlady cleans his apartment. He asks a professor to come to his apartment to view his creation. When he returns to the apartment, however, he finds the lens missing from the flower pot in which he had hidden it. His landlady had watered the pot with the acid he used to shape the lens causing it to disintegrate.

As noted above, the story had also been adapted for an episode of Wyllis Cooper's *Escape* television series. The original story focused on a young man who enrolls in the New York Academy to study medicine but spends all his time studying specimens under his microscope. He becomes convinced that developing a diamond lens for the microscope would reveal even more detail of his specimens. Jules Simon, a young Frenchman who lives in the apartment above his, suggests that the would-be scientist see a medium, Madame Vulpes, who may be able to reveal to him the answers to questions he has about improving the effectiveness of the microscope.

During a session with the medium, she reveals the name of the father of the instrument and confirms that a 140-carat diamond could form the universal lens. After meeting with Madame Vulpes, the self-styled expert on microscopes visits with Simon who indicates he stole a large diamond from a gang of slaves in Brazil. He decides to take the diamond from Simon after murdering him and make it appear as if Simon committed suicide. He is successful in making the murder look like a suicide and having the inquest into the death confirm that finding.

By using a powerful current of electricity, the young man shapes the diamond into the lens he desires. He experiments with a drop of water under the lens. Through the lens, he believes he sees a beautiful woman which he names "Animula." Every day he begins peering through the lens to admire Animula.

Attempting to break his obsession with her, he goes out one evening to the theater. When he returns, he resumes peering through the lens but notices that Animula seems to be fading away. The water had evaporated, and Animula is dying. As the image fades away, the man faints and, in doing so, shatters the microscope. Now, he is thought of as "mad" and lives on charity. He goes by the name of "Linely, the mad microscopist," and is paid by young men's associations to lecture about optics while they laugh at him during the lecture.

"Fisherman's Wife" (aka "Fountain of Youth") – March 21, 1952

Cast: Tom Drake
Jody Parks
Cameron Prud'Homme
Rock Rogers
Maud Scheerer
Writers: Gail & Harry Ingram
Director: Unknown

In a small town in Mexico, a young scientist's chief mission in life is to find the secret to eternal youth. When he believes he has discovered a formula for rejuvenation, a friend's wife, obsessed with the fear of advancing age, agrees to be the guinea pig for his experiment with dire results.

Gail and Harry Ingram were radio and television writers who worked on the television series *Mama* and *The Big Story* among others. Harry Ingram passed away at age forty in March 1952 after suffering a heart attack.

"Flight Overdue" – March 28, 1952

Cast: Veronica Lake as Paula Martin Bennett
Walter Brooke as Don Bennett
Lenore Shanewise as Anna
Thom Conroy as Sam Rutgers
Mary Stuart as Deidre Bennett
Idea from: Jim Lister
Writer: David Davidson
Director: Don Medford

This episode was a thinly veiled fictional story about what happened to Amelia Earhart, the famed aviatrix, whose plane vanished on a flight over the Pacific.

Paula Martin Bennett is a famous aviatrix whose plane supposedly crashed in the Pacific after trying to make a solo flight over the ocean. Her former husband, Don Bennett, married again four years after Paula's disappearance. Nevertheless, he still holds out faith that he will find a full explanation of what happened to his former wife. Hearing strange sounds over his short-wave radio, he believes that Paula may be trying to contact him. Don's current wife, Deidre, is concerned about his continuing fascination with Paula.

Don reminisces about meeting Paula and marrying her only to be disappointed when she begins seeing another man and spending weeks away from him without explanation. He separates from Paula when she won't tell him who she has been seeing or what she is doing. Paula was determined to fly over the Pacific but wreckage was subsequently found on an island when her plane disappeared.

Sam Rutgers, Paula's friend, stops by to finally reveal what happened to her. He explains that he and Paula were associated with the Experimental Projects Bureau attached to the Pentagon. He was the man that she had been seeing. To test her stamina, the Bureau would assign her long flights. The Pentagon had built a rocket launch site on an island in the Pacific and requested Paula to be one of three individuals to pilot a rocket to the moon. After the rocket's launch, it crashed on the moon killing everyone aboard.

While the strange sounds that Don has been receiving on his radio are from the moon, they are not from Paula trying to contact him. The military had dumped plane wreckage on an island to cover-up what really happened to Paula. Hearing the story from Rutgers, Don is glad that his former wife is gone since he says that she only loved herself and now he is free.

In reviewing this episode, Merrill Panitt of *The Philadelphia Inquirer* wrote: "Tales of Tomorrow had better watch out. A repetition of the sort of thing we got in 'Flight Overdue' the other night and all of us science-fiction fans are going to blast jets for another program."

He further commented: "It was a waste of perfectly good talent, to say nothing of her pretty new coiffure, to have Veronica Lake starring in that opus. As a matter of fact, it seems to this casual observer that it's always a waste to spend money on big names for Tales of Tomorrow . . . Right now, we're questioning the decision of the producers to bolster a weak story by casting a movie star in it rather than spend money on a better story."[13]

James Lister, who came up with the idea for this story, was a production coordinator on *Tales of Tomorrow*.

"And a Little Child" – April 4, 1952

Cast: Iris Mann
Frank McHugh
Parker Fennelly
Adelaide Bean
Howard Wierum
Arthur Tell
Writers: Gail & Harry Ingram
Director: Unknown

Not much is known about this installment other than that the tale involved a young girl from the backwoods of Kentucky who discovers that she has the paranormal ability to read minds. She uses that power to save people from a nuclear disaster.

Iris Mann who played the young girl on this episode also starred in the 1952 motion picture, *Room for One More,* with Cary Grant. She later became a free-lance journalist.

"Sleep No More" – April 11, 1952

Cast: Jeffrey Lynn as Bill Garvin
Berry Kroeger as Dr. Samuel Watts
Robert Emhardt
Maxine Stuart as Ellen
Writer: Mann Rubin

Set in the Georgetown section of Washington D.C., Bill Garvin appears at the front door of Dr. Samuel Watts' house near midnight. Bill lives with his wife Ellen just around the corner. He asks the doctor for medicine to keep him awake. The doctor gives Bill a shot of whiskey and asks him why he must stay awake. Bill says that his sleep has become a weapon that can destroy earth.

A few nights earlier, Bill arrived home late from a dinner he attended to honor his associate Dr. Sigmund Baller, a physicist with whom Bill works. When he fell asleep, he dreamt of walking through space in answer to a call. He encounters Lippo who has been trying to reach him for a long time. Lippo wants someone with imagination to lead him and his followers into Bill's world. In his dream, Bill helps Lippo come to earth.

Later, Bill has another dream about Lippo asking him to help his friends cross into Bill's world. If Bill refuses to comply, Lippo says he will sleep for an eternity. Bill helps three of Lippo's followers cross the bridge into this world with each of the beings taking the place of an important man in a position of authority on earth. Lippo says that for every human thriving on earth, there is one of them to take their place. Bill's dreams are the beings' invasion route.

Dr. Watts attempts to tell Bill that his dreams are not real – that he is tired and needs to rest and that Lippo is a figment of his imagination. Bill relates what happened to him this afternoon at work. He saw General Harper lock important papers in his brief case, but the General was really Lippo. Bill protested to a guard that Harper was not who he said he was. Lippo advises the guard that Bill is mad. The guard tells Bill to leave work early and go home to rest.

Bill pleads with Dr. Watts to keep him awake during the night. The doctor gives him some medication that turns out to be sleeping powder – not a stimulant. Lippo appears again in Bill's dreams saying that he has failed him and commands that he sleep for eternity. The doctor, thinking Bill is asleep, checks his pulse but can't find one. Bill is dead.

According to Mann Rubin, he had just gotten out of college when he went to work for *Tales of Tomorrow*. As he explained, "…a friend of mine told me they heard about a new series, *Tales of Tomorrow*, on ABC. I looked in the phone book and went over to the office of George Foley and left three scripts that I had written on spec." He went on to say, "…Monday morning the phone rang about 9:30, … Mr. Foley wanted to see me as fast as possible. By ten o'clock, I was in his office, and he told me he was buying all three scripts."[14]

"Time to Go" – April 18, 1952

Cast: Sylvia Sidney as Natalie Davis
Ed Peck as Michael Davis
Robert Harris as Mr. Tickton
Truman Smith
Vera Massey
Writer: Mann Rubin
Director: Don Medford

"Time to Go" told the tale of Natalie Davis who receives a letter from a new bank in the neighborhood asking her to become a depositor. She goes to the bank where a Mr. Tickton informs her that the bank is for depositing time – not money. He explains that the bank is run by beings from another planet that need time to rebuild their crumbling civilization. The time deposited by humans is then transferred to the alien planet for its use. She is told that she can bank her saved time with interest adding years to her life.

Natalie decides to open an account but must keep it a secret from everyone including her husband, Michael. Every day she deposits time that she has saved doing her housework and other things. She decides to send her husband's dog to the pound so she can save even more time by not having to feed the canine or bathe it. In reaction, her husband says that he will retrieve the dog from the pound and leave her. Mr. Tickton stops by her house to inform her that his civilization now needs even more time to restore their quickly crumbling civilization. For that reason, he is closing her account and borrowing the remaining time she has to live. Natalie has until midnight to put her affairs in order. Panicked, she attempts to phone her husband to tell him what is happening. Natalie wants him to come home immediately. But, as the clock strikes 12:00 am, a man comes to her door telling her that it is time to go.

This story was another original script by Mann Rubin.

"Plague from Space" – April 25, 1952

Cast: Gene Raymond as Colonel Jeffrey Ward
James Doohan as Sgt. Morgan
Richard Keith
Harry Landers
Philip Pine
Charles Proctor
Alex Alexander

Al Checo
Glenn Styres
Story: Henry Guth
Adapter: Mann Rubin
Director: Don Medford

Colonel Jeff Ward thinks he is about to be relieved of command of an Air Force base because of various problems at the base. A general is due to arrive momentarily to carry out this action. Meanwhile, a space craft is approaching the base. After it lands, the colonel closes the base to all additional flights including the general's flight.

The men on the base examine the space craft and eventually learn it is from Mars. They find a living creature inside. Colonel Ward is informed that the creature is transmitting bacteria that is sickening men on the base who subsequently die. The colonel believes that Mars is engaging in germ warfare with earth. Later, doctors discover that the creature is recovering with a reduction in germs after having transmitted them to members of the base. The colonel wants to make sure that the germs do not leave the Air Force base. He decides, with only thirteen out of 2000 men left, to have a bomb dropped on the base to destroy it.

James Doohan, who appeared on this presentation, later became famous for his role on *Star Trek*.

Evidently, Mann Rubin adapted this tale from a short story by Henry Guth titled, "Doom Ship." The story published in the November 1950 issue of *Super Science Stories* shares only its basic theme with the TV episode. The short story concerns Ensign Lefty Shark on the space ship the Tripoli with an interplanetary crew. The Tripoli is on its way to Neptune with passengers and a cargo. Lefty thinks that a red space craft is following the Tripoli. Other crew members think that he may be hallucinating. Subsequently, the other crew realize that Lefty is correct about the red ship.

Lefty is placed in charge of the engine room during the third watch. He finds another crew member tampering with equipment in the engine room which causes the Tripoli to cease moving. The nearby red ship points its ray gun toward Lefty's space craft and fires.

Lefty puts on a space suit and proceeds through an airlock to make his way to the red ship. He sees the Tripoli's engine restart leaving him isolated in space. Lefty determines that the red ship's crew are pirates. He is able to hold the pirates off since his position in space causes the red ship to be wedged between dimensions. The Tripoli returns to rescue Lefty, but he refuses to leave his position wanting to continue to trap the red ship so it cannot take over the Tripoli. He sacrifices his life to save his ship much like in the *Tales of Tomorrow* presentation where Colonel Ward sacrificed his life and remaining crew members to save earth from the plague.

"Red Dust" – May 2, 1952

Cast: Lex Barker as Kurt
Robert Patten as Duncan
Fred Stewart as Dr. Davidson
Skedge Miller as Charlie
Story: Theodore Cogswell
Adapter: Irving Elman
Director: Don Medford

Four crew members of the Meridian space ship are returning to earth after reaching Alpha Centuri – a planet outside the solar system. Two of the members – Kelly and Schwartz, died on Alpha Centuri and were buried under the red dust that pervaded the planet. The crew found Alpha Centuri desolate with nothing living on the planet.

The remaining crew members discover that the red dust from the planet is all over their clothes and space ship and that it is multiplying and appears to be alive. The two crew members who died refused to take their radiation shots. Dr. Davidson informs the crew that the dust is a radioactive virus and the shots just slow the progress of the virus but can't stop it. The crystals grow inside the body and, when they infect an organ, the person will die. However, with the shots, a person could live ten to fifteen years.

One of the crew named Charlie goes berserk and throws himself through an air lock into outer space after saying the crew is taking death back to earth. Dr. Davidson says that the Meridian cannot return to earth and recommends blowing up the space ship. Kurt, the spacecraft's pilot, pulls a gun on Duncan who also doesn't want the ship landing on earth. Duncan then knocks out Kurt and shoots him. The doctor shoots Duncan. Dr. Davidson communicates with earth telling mission control what was found on Alpha Centuri including the effect of the red dust. He then cuts off all communication as he makes sure that the Meridian doesn't land on earth.

This episode was based on a work by science fiction writer, Theodore Cogswell, who would author several subsequent versions of the story.

Cogswell along with Poul Anderson turned the work into a short story called "Contact Point," published in the August 1954 of *If: Worlds of Science Fiction.*

The story focused on three characters: Kurt Keeler, the pilot of the space craft Arcturus, Duncan Carr, the navigator, and Edward Brian, a biologist. A radioactive green dust is causing the crew who had landed on Alpha Centuri to become sick. Two crew members, Ames and Livingston, have already died from the dust, and a third member, Shirey, has committed suicide. Ames was the first crew member to exit the spaceship and stand on the green dust swirling around him. He had returned to the ship with dust all over his suit.

Brian reports that the dust particles have a structure that he has never seen before. They are alive and keep growing and spreading. While the inoculations given by Brian seem to be keeping the remaining crew alive, he predicts they have only fifteen to twenty years to live. The inoculations slow the growth of the virus but don't eliminate it. Brian advises Kurt that the ship should be taken to the radio contact point with earth so that he can report to the authorities information about the dust.

The spacecraft will land on earth in about thirty-two hours. Kurt believes that, once they land, scientists will find a cure for the effects of the green dust which causes the skin of those contaminated to glow in the dark. Brian informs Kurt that they can't go back to earth since the dust would spread until there is no human being left alive. He wants to inform earth about the problem and then blow up the spacecraft. Kurt ends up shooting Brian. Upon hearing the shots, Duncan returns to the control room and begins arguing as did Brian that earth will be destroyed by the dust. Duncan knocks Kurt unconscious and takes over control of the spacecraft. As Duncan is about to blow up the ship, Kurt regains consciousness and shoots Duncan.

The spaceship contacts Colonel Rudd at Chicago Spaceport who informs Kurt that the Martian Federation has attacked earth. Kurt begins destroying the documentation related to the advanced weapons the crew found on Centuri. He also begins reading the notes left by Brian concerning the green dust. Rudd sends fighters to intercept and shoot down Arcturus. Kurt plans to play tag with the fighter squadrons. He ends transmission to earth reporting that he is seven hundred and eighty thousand miles out with an estimated time of arrival in twenty-nine hours and thirty minutes.

In 1975, with his wife George Rae Cogswell, Cogswell produced a version of the story as a play titled *Contact Point* with the three characters of Kurt Benster, the pilot of the spacecraft Arcturus, Duncan Clark, an astrophysicist, and Paul Davison, an extraterrestrial biologist known as "Doc." The two crew members who died of the dust were named Kelley and Schwartzkopf and a third member, Spencer, had committed suicide.

The rest of the play is like the short story. However, near the end of the play, Kurt contacts a Colonel Wetzel at Chicago Spaceport who informs Kurt that the Eastern Federation has attacked the West and not Martians as in the story. Kurt begins reading the notes left by Doc concerning the green dust. Wetzel sends fighters to intercept and shoot down Arcturus. Kurt plans to play tag with the fighter squadrons apparently thinking that they will focus on his craft instead of fighting each other.

"The Golden Ingot" – May 9, 1952

Cast: Gene Lockhart as Professor Vanya
Monica Lovett as Margaret Vanya
David McKay as Dr. Charles
Theo Goetz as the landlord
Story: Fitz James O'Brien
Adapter: Max Ehlrich
Director: Unknown

Set in France, Professor Vanya is attempting to turn base metals into gold using a special catalyst. His landlord comes by demanding that he pay his past-due rent. When his latest experiment is unsuccessful, he is so discouraged that he drinks poison. His daughter, Margaret, goes next door to get Dr. Charles for help. Dr. Charles saves Vanya from death.

Margaret wants to give her father hope to continue his experiment. She scrapes all her money together and purchases a gold ingot which she places in the oven Vanya uses for his experiment. He is overjoyed when he thinks his latest experiment is a success and wants to produce gold ingots every day until he and Margaret have enough money for life. Margaret takes care of the one gold ingot using it every day in the oven without her father's knowledge. Vanya wants to increase his output to two ingots a day. Margaret asks Dr. Charles for advice. He suggests telling her father the truth. Instead, Margaret continues the ruse and asks Charles for a loan to pay the rent.

Margaret plants the ingot in the oven again. The landlord sneaks in the apartment in the middle of the night and steals the ingot. In the morning, Vanya is conducting another experiment but this time wants to create a giant ingot. The landlord stops by saying that he has yet to receive the rent. Vanya discovers the gold ingot in the oven to be missing and asks Margaret to see all the ingots he has created. The truth comes out. Vanya goes crazy, has a heart attack, and dies. The last ingot he made that is taken from the oven turns out to be real gold.

In April 1952, the producer of *Tales of Tomorrow*, George Foley, announced a "Stars of Tomorrow" contest for women with little or no professional acting experience but who think they can act. Women between twenty and twenty-five years of age were to call the producer's office to make an appointment for an audition. They were to prepare a three-minute scene of their own choice. The winners of the auditions would be given a screen test and a part in a Broadway show along with appearing on an episode of *Tales of Tomorrow*.

Monica Lovett who played Gene Lockhart's daughter in "The Golden Ingot" was the top winner.

Fitz James O'Brien, who wrote "The Diamond Lens" as well as the short story on which this episode was based, emigrated to the United States from Ireland in 1852. He was an early practitioner of science fiction who died at age thirty-five from wounds suffered in fighting for the Union in the American Civil War.

The television adaptation, in general terms, was like the original story by O'Brien but the names of the characters were different, there was no issue of past due rent, and the ending of the story was less fantastic than the television version in that the alchemist did not finally turn base metal into gold.

In the story told from the doctor's perspective, a woman named Marion Blakelock knocks on the door of a local physician asking him to tend to her father. She says that her father, William Blakelock, an alchemist, has met with an accident. The doctor, Dr. Luxor, follows her to an old tenement building and walks up the stairs to the father's laboratory. Blakelock's arms, chest, and part of his face have been scorched from an explosion that occurred in the laboratory.

William Blakelock is concerned that Dr. Luxor not reveal anything he sees in the laboratory and says he has been an alchemist since age twenty-two. Two years ago, he says that he succeeded in turning base metal into gold. Each bar he made he gave to his daughter for safekeeping and believes he has accumulated $14,000 in wealth. When he asked his daughter for the gold bars, she told him that they had been stolen.

Blakelock then went about redoubling his efforts to make more gold. He commands his daughter to retrieve one of the ingots to reimburse the doctor for his services. Reluctantly, she gives the doctor a small ingot. As Dr. Luxor leaves the building, Marion asks him to give her back the ingot. He returns the gold bar thinking that she is horrible for requesting it.

The next day, Marion visits the doctor again and reveals that her father failed at turning metals into gold and was near death over the disappointment. She started saving money from her sewing which supported her and her father and used it to buy a small gold ingot. She employed it every day to convince her father that he could make gold. For two years, the deception continued.

She now plans to tell her father the truth and wants the doctor to accompany her. Marion explains to her father what she has been doing and asks for forgiveness. The father believes that Marion and Dr. Luxor have conspired to come up with the story. The alchemist insists that he will show the doctor, based on what he is working on now, that he can turn base metal into gold. He pours the contents of his crucible into a brass vessel, but it doesn't turn into gold. Marion then shows her father the gold ingot she got from the doctor.

Blakelock staggers toward the ingot and falls on the floor. He is dead.

"Black Planet" – May 16, 1952

Cast: Leslie Nielsen as Ken
Frank Albertson as Walt
Horace McMahon as Max, the detective
Helene Miller as Norma
Writer: Mann Rubin
Director: Unknown

At Mount Hopkins Observatory, two astronomers, Walt and Ken, search for a tenth planet in the solar system. Walt had theorized about such a planet eight years earlier. He is obsessed with the idea. He is convinced that the younger Ken is trying to take credit for the planet's discovery. Ken has his own theories about the planet's emergence, which their assistant, Norma believes are correct. Nevertheless, Walt dismisses them as not being accurate. He argues with Ken over the issue during a visit from Norma's brother Max, a police detective. Walt forbids Ken from re-checking his work that night and leaves with Max.

Ken and Norma, who are romantically involved with each other, discuss the matter. Ken seems quite certain that the tenth planet will emerge that very night. Later, Ken returns to the observatory to check his figures and discovers Walt already there, using Ken's calculations to view the emergence of the planet. The feud between the two becomes violent as Walt tries to strike Ken with a tripod. During the struggle, they end up in front of the telescope's viewing scope. Walt suddenly screams and dies. Ken is arrested by Max for Walt's death based on their prior antipathy as well as confused testimony from Norma. But, Norma does not really believe that Ken is responsible for Walt's death. He and Norma escape from the police and return to the observatory. Ken reconstructs the crime scene as Max arrives. As Max enters, Ken finds the true cause of his colleague's death. During their struggle, the telescope was on and pointing at the tenth planet, which had just emerged from behind Jupiter. Ken discovers that the new planet emits intense gamma radiation, which was focused through the lens and aimed at Walt. The full force of the rays proved deadly to Walt. He died from severe internal burns. Max calls the coroner, who confirms Ken's hypothesis. Max lets Ken go as they view the photograph that the telescope had taken of the tenth planet.

About this episode, Mann Rubin recalled, "An actor named Horace McMahon was playing a detective, and he was supposed to handcuff the hero (Ken), and he's leading him out when the hero is supposed to attempt to escape. On camera, when the hero raised his hand, you could see that he wasn't handcuffed."[15]

Helene Miller was the runner-up in the "Stars of Tomorrow" contest described in the write-up of the previous episode.

"World of Water" – May 23, 1952

Cast: Victor Jory as Dr. Franz Kramer
Nita Talbot as Nicki
Logan Field
Merilee Ruick
Maude Scheerer
Story: M.J. Gorley & James V. McGlinchey
Adapter: Mann Rubin
Director: Don Medford

"World of Water" concerned a mad scientist who creates a solvent that changes solid objects into liquid. Dr. Franz Kramer, a chemist who had a nervous breakdown, has set up a small laboratory in his boarding house room to continue his experiments. He is taken with a young woman, Nicki, who lives in the room across the hall and seeks to earn money to impress her. Upon entering Kramer's apartment, Nicki says his place always smells like a zoo. After asking to marry her and being turned down by Nicki, the doctor becomes more detached from reality. He subsequently receives news that his niece, his only close relative who is a nuclear scientist, has died in a nuclear accident.

Kramer proceeds to use his solvent to create havoc in cities on the East coast. He informs the government that he has planted vials of his solvent all over the Atlantic coast. Only he can stop the solvent from destroying solids and flooding cities. The episode ends with the Feds searching for Kramer to stop his madness.

The Dr. Kramer character had a huge round glass tub about three feet across in his apartment that was supposedly filled with the solvent he created. The tub was rigged with hoses and pumps at the bottom. When the character threw items into the tub, the liquid would bubble to convince viewers it was dissolving the solid objects. The camera would do a close up to show the items hidden by the rising bubbles. Then the camera would cut away while stagehands rushed in and removed the objects so that when viewers saw the tub again it would appear that the items had disintegrated.

During the live broadcast, Victor Jory tossed everything he could lift into the tub. He threw the objects with such force that they loosened the hoses and pumps which came floating up in the tank which the TV audience could see in a close-up shot.[16]

The end credits for the episode indicate that it was based on a story by M.J. Gorley and James V. McGlinchey. No information about these writers or the story they wrote could be found. However, writer Lysander Kemp authored a short story published in the January, 1955 issue of *Amazing Stories* with a similar idea of a scientist developing a magical solution that dissolves everything.

"The Universal Solvent" begins when Professor Gaskell, a retired chemistry professor, goes to his neighbor saying that he has something exciting to show him. He holds up two small flasks. In the flask in his right hand, he has a reddish liquid. The other flask contains a whiteish liquid. With a dropper, he places some of the reddish liquid into a tiny glass cup and on top of that liquid, he places a drop of the whiteish liquid. The drops disappear. The professor proclaims he has created a universal solvent.

He also claims that the solvent has dissolved itself straight to the center of the earth. It can't escape from the center and, therefore, it can't reach anything else to dissolve. His neighbor points out that the one drop will dissolve the entire world eventually. The professor realizes that he may have destroyed the earth. The neighbor leaves, goes to his apartment, and begins calculating how long before the world is dissolved.

"The Little Black Bag" – May 30, 1952

Cast: Joseph Anthony as the doctor
Vicki Cummings as his wife, Angie
Florence Anglin as their neighbor
John Shellie as the pawnbroker
Writer: Cyril Kornbluth
Additional Dialogue: Mann Rubin
Director: Charles S. Dubin

A down-on-his-luck physician hasn't had a patient in months ever since he was drunk before an operation and presumably killed a patient. His wife, Angie, is tired of living in poverty. She wants her husband to earn money anyway he can. The doctor goes to a pawnshop to pawn his black bag. The pawnbroker offers him $20 and another black bag that he has had in the shop for years. The bag contains strange instruments and medications.

When the doctor returns to his apartment, a neighbor comes by with her sick daughter who is suffering from encephalitis. Near death, the doctor says there is nothing he can do. However, he gives the little girl medication from the bag that is labeled for curing an infection. The girl miraculously recovers. The doctor believes that he can perform other miracles with the contents of the bag. His wife says the bag is worth $1 million. Writing on one of the instruments says the patent on the bag was applied for in the twenty-first century and the contents may only be used for ethical purposes by authorized personnel.

The doctor continues to treat patients for two years using the medications and instruments from the bag. The medications seem to refill themselves. The doctor believes that a time machine sent the bag to the twentieth century and that, if it is not used ethically, it will return to the twenty-first century. His wife thinks that anyone can use the bag and be a success.

When the doctor reveals to her that he wants the world to know about the bag, she argues against that and ends up stabbing him. She takes the bag and thinks of changing her name so she can practice medicine using the bag. However, when she opens the bag, the instruments and medications have disappeared.

Florence Anglin, who played the neighbor, in this presentation was paid $165 for her appearance. The contract that she signed also stated: "You agree that you will not ad lib or deviated (sic) in any way from the materials authorized by us to be telecast on the program hereunder."[17] Supposedly this clause was in all the contracts actors signed for the show. Nevertheless, it didn't prevent actors who forgot their lines from ad libbing dialogue to cover their mistakes as Lee J. Cobb did at the beginning of "Test Flight."

The Kornbluth short story on which this episode is based was published in the July 1950 issue of *Astounding Science Fiction*. The story provides a different take on how the doctor received the futuristic medical bag and eliminates the wife character in the TV show, replacing her with a young woman named Angie that the doctor came to know.

Dr. Bayard Full, an alcoholic, had been brought before the Committee on Ethics of the County Medical Society for bilking patients out of money by diagnosing their minor ailments as cancer and then promising cures. Since patients no longer trust him, he spends most of his days drinking.

Meanwhile, Dr. John Hemingway, a general practitioner, at some time in the future, is listening to Dr. Gillis, a physicist, talk about time travel. Gillis invented a time machine. To demonstrate it, he places Dr. Hemingway's medical kit in the machine and sends it back in time. The bag disappears. Gillis says that the machine never returns objects it sends through time.

Dr. Full wakes up in his small room in the slums to find a black bag which he thought he had pawned two years earlier. The bag contains rows of medical instruments and medications with plastic cards detailing how they are to be used. The doctor takes one blue pill from a bottle and miraculously his pain goes away and the tremors in his left leg stop. He contemplates taking the bag to a pawn shop to get money to purchase more booze.

As he leaves his room, a woman from the slums asks him to treat her little girl who has an infected arm. He sees a card in the bag labeled "infection" with a syringe full of medication. After he injects the needle into the girl's arm, she recovers quickly.

The girl's older sister, Angie, accuses the doctor of stealing the bag and threatens to report him to the police unless he gives her half of what he will get from a pawn shop for the bag. The first pawnbroker he goes to refuses to give him any money for such a cheap looking bag. At another shop, the pawnbroker will give him only $1 for the bag.

The doctor and Angie go to a cafeteria where she looks more closely at the contents of the bag. On one item, Angie sees "Patent Applied for July 2450".

A newspaper reporter plans to do a story on Dr. Full since he has now opened a sanitarium and is treating patients. Angie has become his assistant. The reporter poses as a patient thinking that the doctor is up to his old tricks of bilking patients. The doctor diagnoses her with the same problems as did her regular physician. Since she couldn't find any malfeasance on his part, the news article in not published.

Dr. Full, getting up in years, wants to turn over the medical kit to all humanity. Before he tells Angie, she brings in a patient, a widow named Mrs. Coleman, who seeks a face lift. Normally, the doctor would not perform such needless surgery, but this time he makes an exception. After the face lift, Mrs. Coleman pays him $500. The doctor then prepares to tell Angie his plans for the bag. When she hears the plan, she snatches the bag with some of its contents falling to the floor. As Dr. Full bends over to pick up the fallen instruments, Angie plunges a scalpel into the doctor's back killing him. She then takes an incinerator box from the bag and inserts the rest of the cautery knives into the box.

The following day, Mrs. Coleman arrives for another treatment - this time on her neck. The woman is nervous of Angie working on her without the doctor. She wants Angie to demonstrate her proficiency, with the cutaneous series of knives, on her own neck.

Back in the future, a sensor in the medical kit produces a notification that a homicide has been committed with the bag. The bag is made inoperable as Angie uses the cutaneous knife on her throat. The knife shears through major and minor blood vessels. The instruments in the bag become crusted with rust, and the medications decompose.

In addition to serving as the basis for the *Tales of Tomorrow* presentation, "The Little Black Bag" inspired a segment of Rod Serling's *Night Gallery* which aired December 23, 1970.

"The Exile"- June 6, 1952

Cast: Chester Morris
Luis Van Rooten
John Boruff
Vera Massey
Robert Herman
Story: Alfred Coppel
Adapter: Edgar Marvin
Director: Unknown

The description for this episode says that an atomic research scientist enters self-imposed exile after one of his experiments exposes him to radiation causing him to become a danger to anyone near him.[18]

The short story by Alfred Coppel published in *Astounding Science Fiction* (October 1952), relates a much different tale about a man named Francis Cain. As the story describes Cain's life, "His books are screened, his music is distilled, he lives in a never-never land of Q-clearances and security. His wife has been investigated, his friends scrutinized, his thought suspected. He is not free."[19]

Cain, a pilot circa 1960, is driving over a rain-soaked road when he is involved in a horrible car accident. He is near death with multiple injuries. At the hospital, the doctors and nurses save his life and fit him with several prosthetics to replace his limbs, eyes, etc. Dr. Ben Isaacs, a friend of Cain's, explains what happened to him. Medical staff placed a plastic mask over his skull and fitted him with plastic arms, artificial legs, metal claws for hands, and glass lenses for eyes. His life was saved because Cain is so valuable to the country's space competition with the Russians to be the first to go to the moon.

Cain feels more like a robot than a human being. He doesn't need much food or sleep to sustain his life. He feels that he must adapt the best he can to his new body. Cain does not want to participate in the race to the moon. Because he can no longer have the same relationship with his wife that he had before the accident, he tells her to get a divorce. He refuses to see his wife when she visits the hospital.

Nevertheless, Cain is placed into the space ship for the maiden voyage to the moon. It blasts off for a single orbit around the moon before it returns to earth. However, the spacecraft goes off course. Cain refuses to correct the error despite commands from ground control. Mission control tracks the craft until it loses touch. Cain continues into deep space realizing a freedom that he could not experience on earth.

A prolific writer of pulp fiction, Alfred Coppel sometimes wrote under the pseudonyms Robert Cham Gilman and A. C. Marin.

"All the Time in the World" – June 13, 1952

Cast: Don Hanmer as Henry Judson
Esther Ralston as The Lady from the Future
Jack Warden as Steve
Lewis Charles
Sam Loganti
Byron Halstead
Writer: Arthur C. Clarke
Director: Don Medford

In "All the Time in the World," a woman asks a shady businessman, Henry Judson, to obtain a list of valuable art objects for her from a museum. She gives him $100,000 for the task as well as a special accelerator bracelet that speeds up time in a five-foot circumference around him while the world outside the circumference appears to stop. She gives him an extra accelerator bracelet for an assistant. Judson hires a man named Steve to help him. The two go to a museum to collect the items on the list.

After collecting the objects, the woman appears to transport the items to her time. Judson and the woman go back to his office. She says that she is returning to her time for safety. He wants to keep the bracelet accelerator for his own use. She says it will continue to operate for as long as he lives and allows him to keep it.

The woman says she came here from 1000 years in the future in order to save mankind's treasures before it is too late. She shows him a newspaper headline about an H-bomb test that she says will destroy earth. If he turns the accelerator on, the world will continue for him in suspended animation, but he will be alone. If he doesn't activate the bracelet, he and the rest of the world will be destroyed. He doesn't know what to do, but he has all the time in the world to figure that out.

The Arthur Clarke short story on which the episode is based was first published in *Startling Stories,* July 1951. At the center of the story is Robert Ashton who is visited by a woman offering him a job and preparing to pay him any sum he wants. She presents a list of the items she wants taken from the British Museum. Like in the TV episode, the woman shows him a bracelet of silvery metal with a series of dials and switches molded into it. The device accelerates time making those outside a seven-foot radius of him appear to be in suspended animation.

Ashton tries to recruit Tony Marchetti to help him with the heist but learns from Aram Albenkian, a crooked art dealer, that Tony is working on a job for him. Albenkian has a device like Ashton's and theorizes that the people who gave them the accelerators are from another world who want to systematically loot earth's treasures.

Since Tony can't join Ashton in the theft from the museum, Ashton recruits Steve Regan and gives him a spare accelerator. They take the items on the list as well as a few for themselves.After the items have been placed in a pile outside the museum, the woman appears and takes the items. She then asks for the accelerators back. She explains that she needed Ashton's help in getting the items so that her limited transporting facilities would not be wasted.

Ashton gives the woman the spare accelerator but not the one on his arm saying that he will reduce his $1 million pound request for payment for the job if he can keep the accelerator.

The woman reveals that she is from the future and that in the future beings can send their minds back in time but not their bodies. She has borrowed the body Ashton sees from someone else. She tells him that he can keep the bracelet and that Ashton's world will end soon.

A super-bomb test will soon occur on earth. It will have the energy of all the earthquakes since the beginning of time and destroy the earth. Before the test occurs, beings from the future are trying to save what they can of the world's treasures.

Ashton faces a choice. He can live out the remainder of his life in isolation from everyone and everything being in suspended animation with the device turned on or else he can witness the last seconds of history if he switches off the time accelerator.

About this story, famed science fiction writer Clarke indicated that it was the first of his stories to be adapted for television. He further commented, "Although I worked on the script, I have absolutely no recollection of the programme, and can't imagine how it was produced in pre-video tape days!"[20]

Arthur C. Clarke, one of the Big 3 of science fiction writers along with Isaac Asimov and Robert Heinlein, co-authored the screenplay for the film, *2001: A Space Odyssey* as well as the sequel *2010*. The photograph shows Clarke working in Sri Lanka on a Kaypro II computer relaying information to Peter Hyams in Los Angeles about the production of *2010*.

"The Miraculous Serum" – June 20, 1952

Cast: Lola Albright as Carol Williams
Richard Derr as Dr. Dan Scott
Louis Hector as Dr. Bache
Peggy Allison as the Nurse
Story: Stanley G. Weinbaum
Adapter: Theodore Sturgeon
Director: Don Medford

Dr. Dan Scott has created a serum that affects the pineal gland making creatures easily adapt to new circumstances. He wants to experiment on live humans. Dr. Bache, his boss, won't permit that unless the subject is near death.

A woman named Carol Williams appears to be at death's door and is given Dr. Scott's serum. She miraculously recovers and is invited to meet with Dr. Scott and his boss. She begins feeling invincible and, as part of her adaptation to her new circumstances, she starts stealing money and seeking power over others. Her adaptive mechanism is out of control.

Dr. Bache wants to operate on her to make her more in control of her impulses. He suggests that carbon dioxide be pumped into her room while she is sleeping to make her unconscious so that the operation can proceed. When she passes out, the surgery is performed. Recovering, she says she will repay the stolen money. But in the final scene, a newspaper article appears saying that the operation was not a success and that she is in jail.

The episode was based on Stanley G. Weinbaum's story, "The Adaptive Ultimate" published in *Astounding Stories* – the November 1935 edition. In the story, Dr. Dan Scott creates his miraculous serum with putrefied bodies of fruit flies injected into a cow. Kyra Zelas, suffering from tuberculous, is the patient that he uses for his experiment on humans. She becomes disease free.

The character of Kyra Zelas is eviler than in the television episode. Upon release from the hospital, she picks up a large stone in the park, slugs a man killing him, and steals his money.

Doctors Scott and Bach attend her trial. When she appears in court, her appearance has changed. She has gained weight, and her hair and eyes are lighter. On the stand, Kyra says that another woman thrust an empty wallet into her hand. The judge dismisses the case. When reporters in the courtroom take her photo, the photo shows her with dark hair as she looked originally.

After the doctors take her back to Dr. Bach's home, she admits that she killed the man. Dr. Scott theorizes that his serum increased Kyra's adaptability to the nth degree with sunlight making her hair and eyes appear lighter and her skin darker. The doctors believe that Kyra is a human mutation.

Subsequently, Kyra leaves the house again. When she returns, she confides that she killed a child in a hit and run accident with a car that she had stolen. The following day, Kyra steals the doctors' money and leaves. Weeks pass. The newspapers report that she is dating the U.S. Secretary of Treasury. She eventually returns to Dr. Bach's house where she starts talking about becoming an Empress.

As in the TV episode, the doctors perform surgery on her pineal gland after making her unconscious with carbon dioxide. Kyra returns to a normal existence.

Science fiction writer Stanley G. Weinbaum, penned the popular story, "A Martian Odyssey" in 1934 a year before he died at age thirty-three from lung cancer.

"Appointment on Mars" June 27, 1952

Cast: Brian Keith as Jack
William Redfield as Bart
Leslie Nielsen as Robbie

Writer: S.A. Lombino
Director: Don Medford

Three private citizens, Jack, Bart, and Robbie, from the United States land on Mars. Their mission has been subsidized by a mining corporation with which they have agreed to share any profits from mineral deposits. On Mars, the three men, wearing coveralls, camp out in a tent. The planet seems almost like earth although they have found no intelligent life – only some plants and a howling wind. Exploring for minerals, they discover rich uranium deposits. They believe they will be wealthy when they return to earth.

Nevertheless, Jack comes down with a headache and begins arguing with Bart. Bart becomes paranoid thinking that he is being watched. The two begin fighting with each other. Bart believes that Jack stole his lucky rabbit's foot. Robbie separates the two from their brawl, but they refuse to turn over their guns to him.

They try to sleep. Bart wakes up thinking that he sees a Martian and begins shooting. He ends up killing himself in a fight with Robbie. Jack says that it was not an accident and pulls his gun on Robbie. He shoots Robbie. Robbie tries to shoot back but drops his gun, and they fight to the death. As they both die, two Martians comment on how quickly the three humans perished.

Producer Mort Abrahams indicated that:

> What happened at the end of the show was that Leslie was supposed to pull a gun on Keith, but the gun fell out of his holster so he didn't have a gun. I stood, I'm sure, pale, and shaking in the control room with the director, and I remember Don and I looked at each other, our hearts in our mouths, wondering how this thing was gonna end. Being consummate professionals, they simply went after each other, hand to hand, which wasn't in the script at all, and remarkably

> ended their fight with a mutual death, exactly when the program should have concluded.[21]

If one views the kinescope of this presentation, it appears that Leslie Nielsen's gun does not fall from his holster. Rather he seems to drop his gun and then wrestles with Brian Keith.

The episode was very loosely based on a short story by Salvatore A. Lombino written under the pseudonym, Evan Hunter. Set in 1989, the story, "What Price Venus?" relates the tale of Tod Bellew and Fred Trupa, nicknamed "Trooper," who are summoned to the Office of the Military by Leonard Altz, Commander, Earth Seven. Earth Seven includes the United States, Canada, Mexico, South America, and England. Both men are informed of a mission to Venus to find a specific seed that the Venerians are reluctant to give up. The two men are made to look like beings from Venus – tall with blue hair and blue skin. The seed they are searching for is small, pale blue in color with a thin network of fibers under a translucent covering.

Bellew and Trupa travel to Venus and are dropped from their space ship onto the planet. After divesting themselves of their helmets and space suits, they begin looking for the small blue seed among the flora in the jungle where they landed.

They come upon a village and meet a native named Ragoo who asks them to stay for a while until the "Planting." While searching for the seed, they find a yellow-flowered plant whose tendrils wrap around Trooper. He attempts to free himself but cannot. Bellew is finally able to free his mate by biting into the tendrils.

They return to the village and notice that the Venerians never seem to eat. The main activity of the men in the village is to go into the jungle and return with fresh soil every day to place on a mound in the center of the village. The men intermittently thrust their hands into the mound seemingly as a religious ritual. The mound of soil is the feeding spot for the Venerians.

Bellew and Trooper are also surprised that they see no children in the village. The natives begin building a large rectangle with new soil to begin the "planting." The "planting" involves the men of the tribe removing glowing spheres from the necks of young woman and planting them in the large rectangle. Tod Bellew and Trooper realize that the Venerians are really plants and that Commander Altz wants the two to bring back seeds that grow into people. The seeds would form the nucleus of a new group of warriors to become part of Earth Seven's army to take over the rest of the planet with its headquarters in Earth Seven.

Bellew and Trupa return to earth and meet Altz. They take out their blaster weapons and kill the Commander. They then take off in a space ship to discover other worlds.

The story was first published in the August-September 1951 edition of *Fantastic Universe*. Evidently, Mars was considered more familiar to television viewers than Venus and so the locale for the TV episode was changed along with the story line. Under the name Evan Hunter, Lombino also wrote *The Blackboard Jungle* and, using the name Ed McBain, authored the *87th Precinct* series of novels.

"The Duplicates" – July 4, 1952

Cast: Darren McGavin as Bruce Calvin
Cameron Prud'Homme as Dr. Johnson
Patricia Ferris as Frances
Alexander Lockwood as Gorham
Writers: Robert M. Simon and Mann Rubin
Director: Don Medford

The subject of alternate worlds was addressed on this episode of *Tales of Tomorrow*. Bruce Calvin, an unemployed engineer, answers a newspaper ad for a mysterious job. He interviews with Dr. Johnson of the Atomic Energy Control to participate in a special experiment that will last three weeks. In return, he will receive $250,000. Johnson tells Calvin that he has been under observation for a year to ensure his qualifications for the experiment.

Dr. Johnson divulges that in a matter of weeks contact will be established with another planet. Life on that planet is identical to life on Jupiter where Johnson and Calvin live. Calvin is to board an automated space ship to earth to stop the exact duplication of human beings on the two planets by poisoning his duplicate on earth. Calvin ultimately agrees to the mission.

Calvin must plant the poison in the duplicate's house so that he will eat or drink the substance. He blasts off to earth where he soon finds his duplicate's house and places the poison in a bottle of liquor in the living room.

He subsequently returns to Jupiter and is given a check for his work. Going home to see his wife, Calvin takes a drink from the liquor bottle on his coffee table. His wife informs him that she saw him in the living room last evening. Turns out that while Calvin was on earth, his duplicate was on Jupiter poisoning his liquor. Calvin dies as presumably does his duplicate on earth meaning that the duplication on the two planets continues.

This episode appears to be the only writing credit for Robert M. Simon.

"Ahead of His Time" – July 18, 1952

Cast: Paul Tripp as Sam Whipple
Ruth Enders
Theo Hathaway
Arthur Tell
Writer: Paul Tripp
Director: Unknown

In New York City in 2052, the world stands on the edge of doom with radioactivity on earth increasing at such a rate that everyone will soon perish. The radioactivity is due to a scientific experiment carried out in 1952 when a scientist discovered a new element. With it, he created a chain reaction, after making a small error, leading to an increase in radioactivity over a one-hundred-year period. Soon the radiation levels will end human life.

A scientist named Dr. Jarvis, in 2052, using a teletimer set to review the past one hundred years, identifies a person who was alive in 1952 and might be able to correct the error. The man's name is Sam Whipple. Whipple has finally perfected his time machine. He transports himself to Dr. Jarvis' office in 2052 where the doctor explains the problem facing the world. Whipple returns to 1952 to attempt to correct the mistake. When he goes to the scientist's lab to point out the error, the scientist doesn't believe him. Sam ends up burning the paper with the calculations for the experiment on it thus saving the future world. Whipple tries to return to 2052, but his sister has destroyed his time machine so that he no longer, in her opinion, wastes his time.

Paul Tripp, who wrote this story, was a musician, actor, and author primarily of children's TV shows. He created the character of Sam Whipple which he also portrayed in a 1966 motion picture, *The Christmas that Almost Wasn't*. The film concerned a bad-tempered millionaire named Phineas T. Prune who purchases the North Pole with plans to evict Santa Claus unless past due rent is paid by Christmas Day. The character of Sam Whipple is Santa's lawyer in the movie.

Paul Tripp also wrote and starred in another episode of *Tales of Tomorrow* in season two titled "Double Trouble." See below.

"Sudden Darkness" – August 1, 1952

Cast: Olive Deering
Robert F. Simon

Mike Keene
Robert Peck
Writer: John Cole

A scientist has developed a device that can shut down all the world's electrical power. All the lights in a small town go out plunging the community into almost total darkness. An embittered woman uses the blackout to further her schemes.

The only other credit that could be found for writer John Cole was for an episode of the early TV anthology, *The Web*. He wrote the presentation, "The Dishonorable Thief," about a mild-mannered private detective.

"Ice from Space" – August 8, 1952

Cast: Edom Ryan as Major Dozier
Raymond Bailey as Congressman Burns
Michael Gorrin as Dr. Meshkoff
Paul Newman as Sergeant Wilson
Writer: E. H. Frank
Director: Don Medford

The experimental AR 76 rocket, designed for manned space flight, blasts off on a test flight and then disappears. The rocket contained mice to determine how living beings experience outer space. Subsequently, the rocket is found on a ranch owned by the Baker family. Congressman Burns of the House Investigating Committee is being briefed by Major Dozier about the project with the Congressman complaining about the cost of the endeavor. When the rocket is examined, a large block of ice is found inside with the mice frozen to death. The ice has a molecular structure different from anything on earth. The entire area in which the ice is stored becomes extremely cold. A military officer guarding the ice freezes to death.

Major Dozier places the entire area and personnel, including the Congressman, under quarantine.

Seventy-five miles of desert are now frozen despite it being summertime. The ice becomes more active emitting radiation. The military is concerned that it will soon envelop a town nearby. The scientists believe that the block of ice may be communicating with others in outer space to invade earth for its warmth.

Major Dozier must decide what to do with the ice. The Congressman continues to point out the Major's shortcomings when compared to his father's career in the military. The Major decides to board the AR 76 with the block of ice and blast off with it into space thereby saving the earth from another Ice Age.

This episode was actor Paul Newman's first appearance as an actor on television.

"A Child Is Crying" – August 15, 1952

This episode was a re-staging of the August 14, 1951 presentation with the same cast. The episode received the *Galaxy Magazine* science-fiction award for the best television show.

Season Two of *Tales of Tomorrow*

"A Bird in Hand" – August 22, 1952

Cast: Henry Jones as Mervyn
Aina Niemela as Edith Holden
Peter Munson as Buddy Holden
Vera Massey
Harry Kersey
Cecile Roy
Writer: Mann Rubin
Director: Unknown

Siblings Edith and Buddy Holden go to their local zoo to see the new bird house. The jittery bird keeper, Mervyn, is reluctant to let them inside. Nonetheless, the kids sneak in but are disappointed to find the bird house nearly empty. They spy one unremarkable-looking black bird in a cage before they are told to leave. The siblings later go back in to retrieve a lost toy. They witness the black bird, in a cackling voice, tell the nervous Mervyn that it has used its powers of mental transference to control all species of animals including insects.

The bird has organized the animal kingdom in a revolt that will eradicate human beings. The bird will begin this evening unleashing a giant swarm of locusts upon the wheat fields of the Midwest. The children go home to inform their parents. Their father refuses to believe them, thinking they have gotten caught up in a game of "Rocket Rangers." The father confines them to their room, but the children make a brave attempt to save the world from the evil bird's plot against humanity.

This story is somewhat reminiscent of Daphne Du Maurier's "The Birds" which was originally published in January 1952. Du Maurier authored the short story which served as the basis for the Alfred Hitchcock film of the same title. Set in England in early December, the tale focused on Nat Hicken who worked part-time on a nearby farm - hedging, thatching, and repairing buildings. Hicken notes that birds seem to be more restless than ever during the preceding fall.

One night while in bed, Nat hears tapping on the window. Opening it, something brushes his hand, jabbing at his knuckles, and grazing his skin. He hears the tapping again and when he opens the window a second time, several birds fly straight into his face attacking him. Later, birds fly into the open window in his children's bedroom. He pushes his children into his bedroom with his wife and tries to fend off their attack in his children's room. He ends up killing about fifty small birds.

Living near the sea, the next day, Nat sees tens of thousands of seagulls stretching as far as his eye could see. Listening to the BBC on radio, he hears reports of a vast quantity of birds causing damage and attacking individuals all over the country. The radio announcer admonishes listeners to board up their windows and doors and chimneys to prevent the birds from invading their houses. Nat follows the advice.

Nat is attacked by gulls while on the way back from the bus stop when his daughter returns from school. He decides to have his wife and kids sleep in the kitchen, the most secure room in his cottage. At night, the family hears airplanes trying to clear away the birds with little luck. The birds fling themselves to death against propellers and fuselages causing the planes to crash.

When the ocean tides ebb, the bird attacks seemed to diminish. Lacking sufficient food and fuel for his family, Nat decides to go to the nearby farm where he worked for some provisions. The farm owner is dead and his family missing. Nat and his wife stock up on supplies from the owner's house. There are no more radio broadcasts about the bird attacks – no broadcasts at all. The birds are back again pecking at the doors and windows in his cottage. As he listens to the tearing sounds of splintering wood, Nat wonders what gave the birds the instinct to destroy mankind.

One wonders if Mann Rubin got inspiration for the *Tales of Tomorrow* episode from this Daphne Du Maurier short story.

"Thanks" – August 29, 1952

Cast: Joseph Anthony as Leo Spain
Robert Middleton as Arnold Haft
Helen Warnow as Pearl Murray
Greg Morton
Bob Nelson
Writer: Mann Rubin
Director: Unknown

Leo Spain is auditioning before concert manager Arnold Haft to play at Carnegie Hall. Haft tells Spain that he just doesn't have the magic – the spark, to thrill audiences with his violin. Haft leaves with Pearl Murray for a dinner engagement.

Leo Spain goes to a bar where he sees his neighbor Dr. John Sacks. Sacks wants Spain to have a drink with him. Spain tells the doctor that his violin career is finished. Sacks mentions that he has been kicked out of the Science Academy because his ideas are improbable. Sacks has created a time cabinet and has been able to send objects 2000 years into the future.

The doctor takes Spain to his room to demonstrate his creation. He sends a pot of flowers into the future by breaking down matter into electrical impulses, transmitting the impulses into the future, and then recombining them into their original form. Leo Spain gets his hand caught in the machine searching for the pot of flowers. He is able to extract his hand which he uses to play the violin, but the hand feels strange. Spain realizes that the hand is not his.

Time passes. Spain has a booking at Carnegie Hall since his new hand plays the violin magnificently. Haft is now managing Spain, and Pearl Murray has become one of his biggest fans. She ends her relationship with Haft. Dr. Sacks comes back stage to see Spain. He tells the violinist that he has received a card from the future stating that the time cabinet had severed a hand from a human being. Sacks asks Spain to give back his new hand. The violinist says that he will but not right away.

Late at night, Spain visits Sacks' room. Sacks tells him to get his hand ready for his time cabinet, but Spain now rejects the notion. He beats Sacks severely. Spain then attempts to destroy the time cabinet. He enters inside the machine and begins to pound his fist against the interior. With great effort, Dr. Sacks crawls to the control panel of the time cabinet and turns the switch which sets the cabinet in motion. There is a terrifying scream from inside the cabinet. Knocking is heard on the outside door from the hallway. Two police officers force their way in. They find Sacks has succumbed to his injuries. One of the cops pulls back the door to the cabinet and finds a card with one word on it – Thanks!

Joseph Anthony appeared in a total of four episodes of *Tales of Tomorrow*. He became a noted Broadway and television director as well as an actor.

"Seeing-Eye Surgeon" – September 5, 1952

Cast: Bruce Cabot as Dr. Tyrell
Joseph Holland as Dr. Xenon
Ed Jerome as Dr. Foyle
Constance Towers as Nurse Martha
Writer: Michael Blair
Director: Don Medford

At St. Jude's Hospital, Doctors Tyrell and Foyle argue over the former's medical techniques. Dr. Tyrell is relatively new to the neuro-surgery unit at the hospital. Dr. Foyle is the older chief of the department. Nevertheless, Dr. Foyle is due to operate on an important physicist and asks Dr. Tyrell to assist him.

Dr. Xenon visits Dr. Tyrell and asks him to use a special pair of eyeglasses during the surgery on the physicist. He also tells Dr. Tyrell that Tyrell will be performing the surgery – not Dr. Foyle.

The day before the operation, Dr. Foyle is suddenly taken ill. Dr. Tyrell will be the chief surgeon. Initially, during the surgery, Dr. Tyrell does not wear the special eyeglasses but then has Martha, his nurse, retrieve them from his office. When he puts them on, he can see the minute cellular structure of the physicist's brain differentiating diseased tissue from healthy tissue. The surgery is a success.

Dr. Foyle discusses the surgery with Dr. Tyrell asking him about the special eyeglasses he described in his report. Foyle doesn't believe that Tyrell got the glasses from a Dr. Xenon. Tyrell shows Foyle the glasses, but now they have no lenses. Tyrell says that no one knows if Xenon exists.

Michael Blair, who scripted this episode, also adapted stories for the psychological thriller anthology, *The Clock*, in 1949 and 1950.

"The Cocoon" – September 12, 1952

Cast: Jackie Cooper as Tom Pearson
Edgar Stehli as John Blankfort
Edith Fellows as Susan
Writer: Frank De Felitta
Director: Don Medford

As one newspaper described this episode, "How does a huge, mysterious cocoon, found by a young girl and two geologists, threaten the destruction of the world? What monstrous, other-world creature escapes from the 'empty' cocoon? What terrifying discovery threatens the life of one of the geologists when his associate decides that the monster must be kept alive?"[22] A horrible invisible creature emerges from a large Paleozoic cocoon found by Susan and her geologist uncle John Blankfort along with Tom Pearson, a young geologist.

About this installment, writer Frank De Felitta said, "At that time, *The Thing* (a movie) was out. I saw it, and came up with an idea for a show that would be like *The Thing*. I called it 'The Cocoon,' which I wrote patterned after *The Thing*. There was an object from another world, there was an invisible creature, and I had an awfully good time writing it."[23]

Evidently, De Felitta had so much fun writing this episode that he wrote a sequel titled "The Fury of the Cocoon" – the March 6, 1953 installment of the series. Unlike "The Cocoon," a kinescope of "The Fury of the Cocoon" still exists.

"The Chase" – September 19, 1952

Cast: Walter Abel
Louise Buckley
Ed Peck
Frank Tweddle
Thom Carney
Writer: Mann Rubin
Director: Don Medford

According to the script for this episode, the installment opens on a young man and woman skiing near High Mount Ski Lodge. The woman is Jane Trousdell, the daughter of Pop Trousdell who runs the lodge. The man is Sander Spence who just arrived at the site before it has officially opened for the season. Sander has trouble unbuttoning his ski jacket since he usually wears a uniform. He tells Jane that he is a scientist taking a brief vacation.

Another guest, Mr. Smith, has just checked into the lodge. Sander thinks it is strange having another guest there before the regular ski season. Jane introduces Sander to Smith who starts asking Sander about where he is from. Sander provides evasive answers.

When Smith leaves the room, Sander bangs his fist against the table in an expression of anger. He says that Smith is "one of them." He reveals to Jane that he is in danger and is being hunted. Sander divulges that he has escaped from the year 2452, a time dominated by machines that have made slaves of all humanity and where there is no freedom. He says that he is a scientist of the state helping to build weapons that keep people enslaved. In his spare time, he constructed a time machine which brought him to 1952.

Every time someone attempts to escape from 2452, Deputies are sent to bring them back. He asks Jane to search Mr. Smith's room to find an identity card. She agrees to help him. Sander reveals that he has a gun. While Jane is searching the room, Sander confronts Smith outside saying that he knows why Smith is at the lodge.

Smith asks Sander what this is all about. He claims that he is not chasing Sander. When Jane calls for Sander, Smith tries to grab his gun. Sander fires killing Smith. Jane says that Smith wasn't a Deputy from the future – but a writer gathering material for a new book about skiing. Sander doesn't believe her and searches Smith's body for a metal bracelet what would identify him as a Deputy.

Sergeant Arthur Bell, a police detective, arrives at the lodge to investigate the murder. Jane believes that once the authorities know who Sander is and where he came from, they'll understand why he killed Smith. She tries to tell the detective that Sander is a fugitive from time. She finds a metal wrist band on the detective that signifies he may be a Deputy from the future. Bell denies the accusation. Jane attempts to inform Sander. Bell tells Jane that she is wrong about him and claims that Sander is the real Deputy from the future searching for him.

Sander appears with his gun. Bell asks Sander to tell the truth about him trailing Bell for months. Sander rolls up his sleeve revealing a metal band. He says that he traced Bell to the area and knew he was a police officer. He got Bell to come to the lodge by murdering Smith. Sander says that life is good where he came from if people conform.

Sander says that he has completed his mission and will return to the future with Bell tonight. Bell picks up the camera he was using to photograph Smith's body, explodes a flash bulb in Sander's face, and then knocks him out. Jane tells Bell to flee. Outside there is a loud, thunderous sound. Jane instructs Bell to put on his skis.

Sander recovers and then goes after Bell with his gun blasting. Rumblings of an avalanche are heard. Jane tries to tell Sander to stop shooting. Sander runs, but the avalanche overwhelms him and presumably Bell gets away.

Don Medford, who helmed more episodes of *Tales of Tomorrow* than any other director, later directed five episodes of *The Twilight Zone.*

"Youth on Tap" – September 26, 1952

Cast: Robert Alda as Jeff
Harry Townes as Dr. Platan
Mary Alice Moore as Kitty
Bernard Burke as a gunman
Ralph Porter as a bartender
Writers: Mann Rubin & Lona Kenney
Director: Don Medford

Jeff is planning to marry Kitty, a waitress at a diner. He needs $1000 to buy a gas station to earn a living.

Dr. Platan offers Jeff $1000 in return for a pint of his blood, type A. The only string attached to the offer is that Jeff will be connected to electrodes around his brain while giving the blood.

Jeff goes to Platan's apartment/laboratory where the doctor says that he suffers from a disease that requires "young" blood. Jeff experiences pain with the electrodes on his head and passes out. The doctor gives himself a transfusion of Jeff's blood. Jeff finally recovers from the experience and sees that the doctor looks much younger than before. The doctor says that he is really 160 years of age.

A previous blood donor comes to the doctor's apartment with a gun saying that he has aged considerably and looks twice his age. The donor wants his youth restored. The doctor advises the donor to get Kitty, Jeff's girlfriend, to donate blood. In the meantime, Platan says that he will restore Jeff's youth with Kitty's blood. When she arrives at the apartment, the doctor takes her blood and gives it to Jeff. Jeff's youth is restored, and Kitty is all right. The doctor won't treat the older donor who still wants the blood from Jeff or Kitty. Jeff is able to get the gun from the donor and turn Dr. Platan over to the police.

Lona Kenney, the co-writer of this episode, was an opera singer. This was the first script she sold for television.

"Substance X" – October 3, 1952

Cast: Vicki Cummings as Selena
James Maloney as Carmichael
Will Kuluva as Samuel
Charlotte Knight as Paula
Writer: Frank De Felitta

Selena is approached by a Mr. Carmichael, a business consultant, to find out what people in her home town have been eating ever since the general store closed with no other grocers around. For a large compensation, she returns to her mother still living in the town to find out what the townspeople subsist on. Selena is surprised that her mother looks ill and the house is in shambles. A scientist named Samuel has been providing all the residents with a dry cake-like substance called "X" which tastes like anything the consumer wants to eat. Samuel reveals that the substance is made by him from sea water and that whatever the eater wants, the brain sends a transmission to the consumer's taste buds that makes substance X taste like the food they desire. The one side effect is that everyone who consumes the substance loses their ambition since they don't have to worry about having enough to eat. Samuel wants Selena to stay in the town to help him build up the residents' sense of pride. Selena decides to leave. She reports what she found to Carmichael who gives her a steak dinner. The steak tastes like it has been poisoned. She finds that she can't eat anything other than substance X. All other food is unpalatable. She returns to her home town for more substance X.

About this original story, writer Frank De Felitta indicated that:

> I was very happy with that one. It was originally called "Manna," like in *Exodus* when God gave them manna, and they keep calling the substance manna throughout the picture. This daughter comes down to town to investigate it, and ends up trapped, she needs it. It's almost like a drug that was created, an allegory for dope that you couldn't even reference on TV any other way...we were sneaking that kind of thing past the censors long before Rod Serling came along with the *Twilight Zone*.[24]

"The Horn" – October 10, 1952

Cast: Franchot Tone as Arthur Martenson
Stephen Elliot as Jake Lippitt
Barbara Joyce as Evelyn Heinkle
Joe Latham as Max Heinkle

Writer: Alan Nelson
Director: Don Medford

Arthur Martenson has been working on an instrument that uses ultrasonic waves to communicate emotions. A fellow employee at the corporation where Martenson is working, Jake Lippitt, complains to the company head, Max Heinkle, that Martenson's work on his invention is interfering with the company's production schedule. Martenson contends that it is not, that the work on his creation is done outside normal business hours. He tells Heinkle that he will complete his invention in two months.

Lippitt wants to marry Evelyn Heinkle, the boss' daughter. But she breaks up with him because he is bitter and arrogant. She has designs on Martenson. Martenson feels that his creation will help people to communicate better.

After two months, Martenson's invention is complete. It looks like a French horn to Heinkle. When Martenson plays the instrument, it makes Heinkle feel exhilarated. The horn is designed to relay emotions that people are really feeling. The scientist also demonstrates it on Lippitt by making him fear heights.

Martenson becomes engaged to Evelyn. On the night that he is to demonstrate the instrument before a group of scientists, Lippitt tries to convince him to make money from his invention. When Martenson resists, Lippitt fights with him and takes the horn. Lippitt stands on a balcony railing outside Heinkle's office threatening to destroy the instrument by dropping it six stories. He blows the horn causing Heinkle to aim a gun at Martenson, but Heinkle turns the gun toward Lippitt who falls with the horn to his death. Martenson says that he will not try to make another horn.

Alan Nelson published "The Gaulcophone," the basis for this episode, in *The Magazine of Fantasy & Science Fiction* dated August 1952. The main character's name was Arthur Gualco who was employed at the Heinkle Music Works. Gualco has a condition known as hyperacusis – an abnormal acute sense of hearing and a painful sensitivity to sound. He can hear the heartbeats of everyone in the same room with him. He wears a "sound diminisher." Any loud noises can cause Gualco to suffer from noise poisoning.

After work, Arthur spends hours developing a special instrument. Everyone, including Heinkle's daughter, Evelyn, likes Arthur except for Jack Lippitt, the shop foreman, who is jealous of Arthur's special talents. Evelyn has fallen in love with Arthur Gualco.

Gualco completes his Gualcophone which communicates to others the emotions of the person playing the instrument. Listeners hear nothing, but they feel something. Gualco intends for his creation to bring people closer to one another.

The ending of the story is quite different from the television episode. Heinkle decides to have Leon Mazzano, a violin virtuoso, debut the instrument during one of his concerts. The violinist plays the Gualcophone right before intermission. When he begins playing, there is no reaction from the audience. They simply become bored and restless. Mazzano has no real emotions except for boredom and self-love.

Gualco decides to play the instrument himself, but Heinkle believes the audience applause will kill Gualco. Heinkle attempts to demonstrate the instrument before the thousands in attendance. He fears appearing in front of such a large group of people and communicates this when playing the Gualcophone. He then feels anger at how the audience reacts to his performance. The crowd responds with fear and hate and begins to yell 'kill him!"

Gualco comes onto the stage, pulls the instrument from Heinkle, and collapses at the noise from the audience. Evelyn picks up the Gualcophone and begins playing it sending love and tenderness throughout the concert hall.

The noise poisoning almost finishes Gualco, but, after three months, he recovers. He marries Evelyn. Heinkle locks up the Gualcophone in a safe in the basement of his shop.

Apparently, Alan Nelson wrote only short stories which were published in *The Magazine of Fantasy & Science Fiction* as well as in *Weird Tales* and *Cosmopolitan.* He passed away in 1966.

"Double Trouble" – October 17, 1952

Cast: Ruth Enders
Paul Tripp
Ferdi Hoffman
Raymond Bailey
Harrison Dowd
Frank Marth
Joseph Abdullah
Story: Paul Tripp
Adapter: Armand Aulicino
Director: Unknown

A science fiction writer authors a story about a death ray machine. Coincidentally, he finds that the government really has created such a machine and seeks to keep it a secret.

This was Paul Tripp's second appearance on the series. Ruth Enders, his co-star, was Mrs. Paul Tripp.

"Many Happy Returns" (aka "Invaders at Ground Zero") – October 24, 1952

Cast: Gene Raymond as Andy
Flora Campbell as Jane
Clifford Sales as their son Jack
Edwin Cooper as neighbor, Dr. Barnes
Richard Trask as Peter
Story: Raymond Z. Gallun
Adapter: David Karp

Director: Don Medford

Andy is working on projects in the basement with his son, Jack. Jack has developed his own electrical device and mentions to his father that a Mr. White has told him how to construct the apparatus consisting of several metal coils.

That evening, Andy goes down to the basement and touches the device his son built. It sends a shock through his body knocking him to the floor. He says that it has enough power to electrocute a man. Jack says that Mr. White communicates to him by mental telepathy. Furthermore, he explains that Mr. White speaks to him from the moon and says that someday he will visit earth. The machine that Jack built is a way for Mr. White to send him photos of himself. Jack shows his father one such picture of an extraterrestrial on the moon.

Jack's mother, Jane, is afraid of Mr. White appearing suddenly at their house. Andy warns his son about Mr. White, but Jack doesn't want to talk about him anymore. Jack loses his ability to speak but still can communicate by shaking his head "yes" or "no." He acknowledges that there are other devices like the one he made in the neighborhood constructed by other children. For example, Jack's friend, Peter, has been sending items to Mr. White with the device he built. Andy decides to send Mr. White a booby trap consisting of dynamite to break the control he has over children. After he sends the booby trap, Dr. Barnes stops by to say he witnessed an eruption on the moon through his telescope. Jack gets his voice back.

The episode was based on "Stepson of Space" by Raymond Z. Gallun published in the October 1940 edition of *Astonishing Stories*. While the basic story line is similar to the television presentation, there were some major differences. The device that eight-year-old Jack built was made from a peach basket with tin cans wrapped around the outside and radio wires circling each can and attached in the center of the bottom of the basket to a heavy block of wood.

Andy learns that Jack got the idea for making the contraption from Mr. Weefles, his imaginary friend who communicated to him by mental telepathy. An object drops out of Jack's pocket that is a three-inch cylinder tapered at the end. Removing the end, Andy finds a tiny scroll containing pictures from another world. One photo shows a being looking like an old man wearing a metal helmet. There is also a photo of a large version of the contraption that Jack had made.

Afraid of what he found, Andy takes Jack with him in his vehicle and speeds down the road. They have an accident that severely injures Jack. His father is mostly unhurt. Andy seeks revenge against the alien that directed Jack to create the peach basket contraption. With Jack in the hospital clinging to life, Andy returns home, gets some dynamite, places it inside thermos bottles, and uses his son's creation to hurl the bottles into space.

The next day, the doctor says that Jack's condition has improved. Andy begins to think that Mr. Weefles is responsible for Jack getting better and then believes that maybe the alien wanted to keep Jack alive for his own purposes. Andy leaves the hospital to drive back home now worried about the bottles of dynamite he had hurled into space. But he feels that there is nothing he can do so he returns to the hospital. He hears on the radio reports of volcanic activity on the moon.

Writer Raymond Z. Gallun published his first science fiction stories in 1929 at age sixteen.

"Tomb of King Taurus" – October 31, 1952

Cast: Walter Abel as Dr. Allen
Charles Nolte as Joy Logan
Richard Purdy as Quincy
Writer: Mann Rubin

"The Tomb of King Taurus" concerned an archeological expedition in Egypt headed by Dr. Allen with Quincy, his hieroglyphics expert, and Jay Logan, his laborer. Logan happens upon a shaft leading to the King's tomb. Quincy translates the inscription on the entrance to the tomb which warns no one to open the tomb less they be cursed forever. Of course, Dr. Allen opens the tomb and the sarcophagus inside revealing the King's mummified remains. But the mummy is still alive. Quincy shoots the mummy leading to the King's death. Allen wants to discover how the King stayed alive for 4000 years. Another inscription by the sarcophagus indicates that a special herbal liquid fed to the King through a tube kept him alive. The three men fight over which one of them should drink the remaining liquid with Jay overpowering Quincy and then Allen shooting Jay. Dr. Allen drinks the potion and, as he does, the tomb's door closes trapping the doctor alive for all eternity.

Walter Abel, who appeared as Dr. Allen in "The Tomb of King Taurus," had a lengthy film and television career. He made his movie debut in 1918 and appeared in over sixty films. On television he had roles in series ranging from *Playhouse 90* to *The Defenders* to *The Farmer's Daughter*.

"The Window" – November 7, 1952

Cast: Rod Steiger as Henry
Frank Maxwell as Al
Virginia Vincent as Jean
William Coburn as the father
Merle Albertson as the daughter
Muffet Peter as the secretary
Jim Walsh as the floor manager
Robert E. Levine as the agency executive
Don Medford as the director
Mort Abrahams as the producer
Merle Worster as chief engineer
Roger DeKovan as the announcer
Writer: Frank De Felitta
Director: Don Medford

This installment involved the TV presentation of "The Lost Planet" by the producer which kept being interrupted by phantom broadcasts through a window showing scenes with three people in a kitchen somewhere in an apartment building in New York City. The interruptions present Jean and Al, husband and wife, sitting at their kitchen table with Al's friend Henry. They are talking as Al and Henry drink.

Back to the TV studio, the announcer for *Tales of Tomorrow* apologizes to viewers about the phantom broadcast. The television picture goes back to the apartment with Al insulting his wife and becoming progressively drunker. Al leaves the room, and Jean and Henry hug each other. Back to the television studio, a commercial for Kreisler watch bands airs but is cut short at the end with the broadcast of the kitchen where Henry and Jean are discussing their affair. Henry wants to murder Al and make it look like a drunken accident so he can marry Jean and she can inherit Al's insurance money.

Back at the studio, a written record of the phantom broadcast is made to present to the police. At the apartment, the plan is to push Al out an upper story window at 1:00 am. The TV station crew attempts to locate the apartment building by calling a store which they think is next door, but the store doesn't know the couple. The husband returns to the kitchen and is slugged by Henry. The studio crew contact the police. Back to the apartment, Henry and Jean try to get their stories straight about Al's pending accident. The police arrive at the studio where the crew tells them that tomorrow, when a man falls out of a window, to phone the studio for more details about the man's death.

The story came about when producer Mort Abrahams made a bet with writer Frank De Felitta to write something that could only be presented on live television. "That could not be done in theater, that could not be done on film, and the only medium it could be done is live television. And I bet him a dinner."[25]

The producer, director, and other crew for *Tales of Tomorrow* appeared as themselves in this episode. The concept of characters being presented through a window was the inspiration for a CBS series titled *Windows* created by De Felitta and Mort Abrahams. The series ran from July 8, 1955 to August 26 of that year as a summer replacement for *Person to Person.* Each installment opened with the camera moving through an ordinary window to present stories about people dealing with real problems such as the effects of alcoholism on a person's family and the efforts of an illiterate woman to learn how to read.

"The Camera" – November 14, 1952

Cast: Donald Buka
Olive Deering
Joe Marr
Michael V. Gazzo

Writer: Mann Rubin
Director: Unknown

A photographer discovers a camera that can photograph things as they will be twenty-five years in the future. With a money-hungry wife and a ruthless publisher as a boss, the photographer uses blackmail to rid his life of both using the special camera.

Donald Buka, who starred on this presentation, had a lengthy career on television starring on episodes of series such as *Lights Out*, *Suspense*, *One Step Beyond*, *77 Sunset Strip*, and *Perry Mason*.

"The Quiet Lady" – November 21, 1952

Cast: John Conte
Gaye Huston
Glenn Walken
Una O'Connor
Martin Agronsky
Story: Phyllis Sterling Smith
Adapters: Irwin Lewis & Armand Aulicino
Director: Mort Abrahams

This episode concerns several metallic spheres landing on earth and supposedly spreading a deadly disease. A woman seeks to do what doctors and scientists have been unable to accomplish and save more people from dying. The spheres are trying to tell earthlings how to cure the disease. They are not spreading it.

The presentation was based on a short story by Phyllis Sterling Smith published in the August 1952 edition of *Thrilling Wonder Stories* involving Anna Kemp, an elderly Quaker lady. The story's title is "The Quaker Lady and the Jelph."

The story begins: "Anna knew what it was, of course, as soon as she saw it. The iridescent metal bubble sat lightly upon the pine needles, and the sunlight flickering through the tall trees sent rainbows of color pulsating across its surface."[26] Newspaper reports had noted that three other balls came to earth. They contained invaders from outer space. Creatures, called "Jelphs," emerged from the balls. They were so named because of their resemblance to jelly fish. Jelphs were about a foot in diameter. The Jelph that Anna came upon uncurls its tentacle and presents Anna with a stone that looked like a large opal.

Anna attempts to communicate with the Jelph, and it apparently understands her. She warns the creature that its life is in danger because the word is that they are poisonous since people die in the areas where the spheres land. The Jelph communicates to Anna that it doesn't want to leave and that it came in peace. She places the metal sphere and the Jelph in the hollow of a tree and goes back to her family to tell them what she found.

When Anna arrives at the cabin, the family is listening to the radio reporting that the Jelph invasion is being met with federal marshals hunting them down and killing them. She informs her family about the Jelph she encountered. Her family wants to contact the authorities about her discovery.

Anna returns to the tree where she left the Jelph and thinks that she hears sirens in the distance. She encourages the Jelph to leave. Her grandchild, Annsy, appears warning her grandmother that the police are looking for her. Anna slips the Jelph in her knitting bag and asks Annsy to hide the bag in her bedroom in the cabin. Meanwhile, Anna attempts to lead the police on a wild goose chase with the metal globe in her arms. However, the police catch up with the old lady as she tosses the globe into the nearby lake. They all return to the cabin where Annsy has collapsed like others who had come into contact with the Jelph. Anna grabs her knitting bag at the foot of the couch where Annsy dropped it and reveals the Jelph.

The Jelph indicates that it can cure Annsy. It indicates that the stone that the Jelph had given Anna can help Annsy. The stone is a way that the Jelph's thoughts are communicated to others who place the stone in their mouths or ears. It is a thought receiver.

The stone communicates that the earth passed through a cloud in space that contained poison. The Jelph detected the poison and sent doctors to treat earthlings, but the federal marshals killed all the Jelph medical experts except the one Anna rescued. The Jelph dictates instructions for making an antidote to the poison. Later, the Jelph transports back to the metal ball and it takes off for its home planet.

Columnist John Crosby relates a story about then seven-year-old Glenn Walken who appeared as one of the spheres in the television episode.[27] As a bonus for appearing in the story, Glen received the sphere costume. It was a canvas bag about the size of a beach ball with a foam rubber exterior painted green. Initially, the idea was for Glenn to roll around inside the bag but he never knew which side was up. The bag was unzipped and Glenn was allowed to expose his legs so that he could walk around, instead of roll around.

Glenn Walken is the brother of Christopher Walken.

Phyllis Sterling Smith, who authored the short story for this episode, wrote several fantasy and science fiction tales including "What Is POSAT?" about the Perpetual Order of Seekers after Truth, a secret society.

"The Invigorating Air" – November 28, 1952

Cast: Joseph Buloff
Anne Seymour
Maurice Burke
Martin Brandt
Harry Pederson
Writer: Frank De Felitta
Director: Unknown

A timid bank teller, who aspires to be a scientist, creates a gas that heals damaged tissue and promotes growth in plants and animals. Nevertheless, his shrewish wife is not impressed with his discovery.

Joseph Buloff, who had the lead on this installment, appeared in supporting roles in films like *Somebody Up There Likes Me*, *Silk Stockings*, and *Reds*.

"The Glacier Giant" – December 5, 1952

Cast: Edith Fellows
Chester Morris as Chester Matteson
Murray Tannenbaum as the abominable snowman
Frank Silvera
Virgil Grant
Kaie Deei
Morley Chang
Yuki Shimoda
Writer: David Durston
Director: Unknown

A newspaper reporter accompanies a scientist and his daughter to the Himalayas to investigate reports of a tribe of abominable snowmen. They discover a member of the tribe entombed in a glacier, but the snowmen come to life as a great thaw occurs. During the story, the scientist is killed by an abominable snowman.

Murray Tannenbaum, who appeared as the abominable snowman on this installment, played basketball at Long Island University. He made his video debut on this episode. At seven feet four inches, he had to wear special shoes to build him up to appear eight feet tall.

"The Fatal Flower" – December 12, 1952

Cast: Victor Jory
Don Hanmer
Writer: Frank De Felitta
Director: Don Medford

Two botanists – Dr. Alden and his new associate Merriman, are doing research on plants in the jungle of Brazil. Alden is developing a large carnivorous hybrid flower. His associate is bored living in the jungle away from civilization. He is so bored that he offers Alden $10 for one of the letters Alden just received. The next day, Dr. Alden asks Merriman which letter he chose, but Merriman doesn't want to share anything about the letter.

Alden continues to question his associate about the letter and almost comes to blows with Merriman as Alden's heart gives out and he has to take his medication. Alden subsequently discovers that his carnivorous hybrid has matured to the point that it imbibes on small animals.

Dr. Alden informs Merriman that he will send him back to the States on the next ship and says that it will ruin Merriman's reputation as a scientist. Alden names his hybrid species "Emily" after his wife. Later, Alden decides to give Merriman one more chance to return the letter to him. But Merriman now wants to leave for the United States.

Alden believes that the letter is from his wife Emily whom he thought had divorced him after his eight years in the jungle. Merriman says he has yet to read the letter. Frustrated over the situation, Alden feeds Merriman to the hybrid flower which has been deprived of food for several days. Merriman drops the letter. Alden reads it which says that Merriman was a below-average student and needs discipline. Alden suffers a heart attack and falls next to the ·al flower with predictable consequences.

Don Hanmer appeared on this and two other episodes of *Tales of Tomorrow*. He had a lengthy career as a supporting actor during the last half of the twentieth century with roles on series ranging from *The Untouchables* to *Mission: Impossible* to *Lou Grant* and *China Beach.*

"The Machine" – December 19, 1952

Cast: Georgann Johnson
Gene Lockhart
Writer: Frank De Felitta
Director: Unknown

A doctor possesses a medical device that foretells the future. The device warns the doctor that one of his infant patients will grow up to become a murderer. The infant's mother attempts to steal the machine from the physician.

According to IMDb, this episode was based on a story by John W. Campbell writing under the pseudonym Don Stuart. While Campbell did author a story titled "The Machine," it bears little resemblance to the episode description.

In the story, the machine does everything for everyone in a society of the future. Humans don't have to work, and so they pursue leisure. Tal Mason has created an old airplane to occupy his time. However, the Machine won't permit Tal to fly his airplane.

The Machine subsequently makes an announcement stating that humanity has forgotten how to create things and so the Machine will leave earth and go to another planet.

Tal is informed that he can now fly his airplane. As fear and madness overtake the populace, Tal and his female friend, Aies Falcon, load his plane with provisions and take off. They decide to fly to the Great Lakes region where it is cooler than in Texas where they reside and there will be fewer people in that region. Tal and

Aies travel to Lake Superior near a deserted city. They find shelter. Tal constructs a steam-heating system to keep them warm. Other people begin arriving resulting in nearly 200 couples. They begin building permanent shelters and raising crops. Men from the south seeking food and women also arrive, but Tal and the other men of the community drive them off.

Rather than based on this story, the episode "The Machine," also titled "Keep Out" in some TV listings at the time, appears to be another original teleplay by Frank De Felitta.

"The Bitter Storm" – December 26, 1952

Cast: Arnold Moss as Professor Leland Russell
Joanne Woodward as Pat Barnett
Philip Pine as Pat's friend Steve
Ethel Remey as Pat's mother Madelaine
Warren Parker as the voice of God
Writer: Armand Aulicino
Director: Don Medford

On an isolated island, Professor Leland Russell is experimenting with an advanced radio receiver. Visiting him are his sister Madelaine, the widow of a pastor, her daughter Pat, and Pat's friend Steve. A hurricane-like storm is brewing outside their house. The professor is bitter because he feels that others have profited from his inventions while he has not. He believes his radio receiver will earn him money since it can pick up sounds from history. Demonstrating it, a speech by Franklin Delano Roosevelt is heard. Madelaine then hears a sound from the very distant past. She understands the meaning of the voices, but no one else around her does. She screams and then faints at the sounds.

The storm becomes worse. Steve suggests that they evacuate the house since the trees surrounding the dwelling may come crashing down. He goes to get the launch ready to take them to the mainland. The professor realizes that Steve is risking his life to save them. He turns his machine back on and now understands the voices that his sister had heard. They are voices from the time of Jesus Christ's crucifixion. He also hears the voice of God. Everyone in the room begins to understand the sounds. The Professor regains his faith in people. They all leave the house but do not take the machine with them.

This episode was actress Joanne Woodward's television debut.

"The Mask of Medusa" – January 2, 1953

Cast: Raymond Burr
Steven Geray
Writer: Nelson Bond

This presentation was not an original episode of *Tales of Tomorrow*. Most newspaper TV listings at the time printed "The Mask of Medusa" and not *Tales of Tomorrow* as the program airing in *Tales*' timeslot. This story was in fact a rerun from an episode of the anthology *Stars Over Hollywood.*

"The Mask of Medusa" concerned a convicted kidnapper and murderer who had escaped from prison. In the story, Thomas Cavendish learns from a radio announcement that Milo Shaner, a thirty-five-year-old criminal, is on the loose with police after him. Cavendish, with his daughter Marina, runs a wax museum featuring lifelike models of notorious criminals. He leaves his daughter alone at the museum while he goes out for a newspaper. Milo enters the museum, and Marina, not recognizing him, shows him around the gallery. Cavendish returns and takes over as Shaner's guide. The museum owner explains to the prison escapee that his life's mission is to show murderers in human form. Milo wonders how Cavendish made the wax figures so lifelike. The museum owner says that his next subject will be a man who committed kidnapping and murder.

Milo Shaner comes to believe that Cavendish encapsulates real bodies within his wax forms which the museum owner confirms. He goes on to explain that he didn't kill the murderers – that they killed themselves by looking at the head of Medusa which turned them into stone.

Cavendish invites Milo to look upon Medusa which Marina had discovered in Greece. Since she is pure of heart, viewing the head doesn't affect her. Milo doesn't believe the story. He wants Cavendish to help him get away by threatening Marina's life. He asks Cavendish to place him in a crate and then be shipped aboard a boat. The museum owner says he will need money to do that but ultimately refuses the request. Milo ties up Cavendish who subsequently changes his mind and says he will help him. Marina pulls open a curtain to reveal a coffin standing upright. She opens the coffin to show the mask of Medusa. The next day, Cavendish shows visitors his latest acquisition – kidnapper and murderer Milo Shaner.

"Conqueror's Isle" – January 9, 1953

Cast: Ray Montgomery
Writer: Nelson Bond

As with the preceding episode, "Conqueror's Island," was a repeat of an August 29, 1951 science fiction installment of *Stars Over Hollywood.*

The presentation concerned a story related by a young Navy flier to a doctor after being rescued from a raft drifting in the South Pacific. Lieutenant Joe Brady, on a bombing mission during World War II, hit an enemy ship which exploded sending a piece of the freighter into his plane. Losing altitude, the aircraft is caught up in a typhoon and eventually lands on a secluded island in the Pacific. A group of men, led by Dr. Grove, approach the aircraft and take the three-man crew to an underground facility on the island. The men initially resist getting on an elevator in the facility. The doctor uses a slender pen-like tube to incapacitate them. Grove informs Brady that firearms of any kind will not work on the island. The men are taken to a maze of corridors and each placed in their own cell.

Brady wakes up alone in a locked cell. Dr. Grove appears stepping through a solid wall. Brady finds that the men on the island are superior beings – mutants born of normal parents. Such beings banded together through mental telepathy and took over the deserted Pacific Island. They plan to conquer the world someday. Eventually, regular human beings will become extinct like Neanderthals as higher life forms become dominant.

Brady tells his current doctor that there are two hundred humans in metal cells on the island consisting of men and women who have disappeared over the years in that region of the world. He says that some of the superior beings have already infiltrated other parts of the world waiting to take over. Furthermore, the flier explains that, to prevent such a takeover, the island must be destroyed with an atomic bomb.

The one weakness the superior beings have, according to Brady, is that they cannot willfully cause any creature pain. He says that he escaped the island after asking Dr. Grove to take him to the surface so he could retrieve items from his marooned aircraft. Brady then knocked Grove unconscious and used a life raft from the plane to get off the island. Subsequently, he was rescued by the Navy.

Brady's doctor – Dr. Gorham, listening to the Navy flier's story, says that he will report it to his superiors. Out of the room, Gorham tells another medical officer that he believes Brady is mentally ill. Gorham leaves the hospital by walking quietly through an outside wall.

"Discovered Heart" – January 16, 1953

Cast: Susan Hallaran as Josie
Jim Boles as Stranger

Alfreda Wallace as Rosie
Frank Milan as Frank
Robert Pattem as Phil
William Lee as Captain Hayes
Writer: David Durston
Director: Daniel Petrie Sr.

An extraterrestrial who is scouting for a pending hostile invasion of earth visits a lighthouse hoping to use it as a signaling station. The space alien befriends a young girl named Josie who makes a playmate out of the half fish, half man creature. Due to her kindness and courage, the extraterrestrial surrenders his life to prevent the invasion.

Susan Hallaran McKenzie was ten-years old when playing the lead on this episode. She indicates that "I remember it was fun to do and I enjoyed it."[28]

"The Picture of Dorian Gray" – January 23, 1953

Cast: John Newland as Dorian Gray
Peter Fernandez
Joseph Anthony
Natalie Norwick
Robert Herman
Margaretta Warwick
Story: Oscar Wilde
Adapter: Anne Howard Bailey

While based on the novel by Oscar Wilde, there appears to be no kinescope or script existing for this episode. The original novel focused on Dorian Gray who had a painting done of him by his friend Basil Hallward who was infatuated with Dorian. Dorian believes that beauty and sensual fulfillment are the only worthy pursuits in life.

He sells his soul to ensure that his portrait and not he will age as he grows older. He remains young and attractive while his portrait ages as it records every one of Dorian's immoral behaviors.

Unlike many episodes of the series, "The Picture of Dorian Gray" was set in 1880's London, England, and not in the future.

According to Irving Robbin, the music director for *Tales Of Tomorrow*, different paintings were done for each stage of Dorian Gray's aging process. The final portrait was that of a withered old man. A gush of blood was to ooze from the painting at the position of the heart with the actor playing Gray to clutch his heart and collapse. For fear of staining the portrait with stage blood, the producers did not test the prop before the live broadcast. A stage manager hiding behind the portrait was to squeeze a rubber ball releasing the blood. He squeezed so hard that the stage blood barreled out of the painting right into the camera lens.[29]

John Newland, who portrayed Dorian Gray, would go on to host the speculative fiction series, *One Step Beyond.*

"Two Faced" – January 30, 1953

Cast: Richard Kiley as Paul Amanston and Julio Venichio
Reba Tassell as Lucia
Mario Badolati as Dr. Marciano
Zolya Talma as Mrs. Rossana
Writer: David Durston
Director: Don Medford

What to do when your new wife doesn't love you but loves another? That question is answered on this episode. Lucia tells her mother that she doesn't love her new husband Paul Amanston because she loves Julio, her former lover. Lucia's mother, Mrs. Rossana, responds to her daughter that she should be happy because Paul is wealthy although not the handsomest of men. Paul learns how Lucia really feels about him and that Julio has committed suicide. Dr. Mario Marciano, a friend of Amanston's, claims that he can transplant Julio's head on Paul. Paul agrees to have the operation.

David Durston, who wrote this and other episodes of *Tales of Tomorrow*, had a checkered career in the entertainment industry. He was an associate producer on the TV show, *Your Hit Parade*. He later wrote and produced the cult film, *I Drink Your Blood* about hippies who become rabid zombies and eat people. He also made such movies as *Felicia* (1964) and *The Love Statue* (1965) as well as directing several gay pornographic movies.

"The Build Box" – February 6, 1953

Cast: Glenda Farrell
Joey Fallon
Vaughn Taylor
Jack Davis
William Lee
Writer: Armand Aulicino
Director: Unknown

A young boy is given a box full of old toy buildings by the owner of an old store. The boy's adoptive parents dislike the box, which turns out to be a potential force for counteracting greed and hate in the small New England town in which they live.

Armand Aulicino, who wrote this episode as well as others for *Tales of Tomorrow*, had a varied career in the arts. He was a playwright, author, and lyricist writing the book and lyrics for a 1969 musical drama based on the Sacco-Vanzetti case. In addition, he wrote two cookbooks – *The New French Cooking* and *The New International Cuisine.*

"Another Chance" – February 13, 1953

Cast: Leslie Nielsen as Harold Mason/ Jack Marshall
Virginia Vincent as Carlotta/Regina
Robert Middleton as Dr. John Borrow
Writer: Frank De Felitta
Director: Don Medford

Harry Mason steals a valuable jewel but is unable to fence it because of its notoriety. He hides out in a run-down apartment with his nagging wife Carlotta who threatens to leave him if he doesn't sell the jewel within twenty-four hours. Harry reads a newspaper ad from a Dr. John Borrow stating he can help. When he visits Borrow, the doctor says that he will give Harry another chance to live his life all over again. Borrow has a machine that will make Harry forget his past seven years, but he will still have the ability to start a new life. In return, Borrow will keep the stolen jewel.

Harry sits in a chair with a metal band around his head. He wakes up seven years earlier in 1946 with the name Jack Marshall. Nevertheless, Jack falls back on Harry's old ways of stealing. This time he steals a stack of nonnegotiable bonds. His wife, who looks suspiciously like Carlotta, is named Regina. He again goes to Dr. Borrow, but this time the doctor says that he can't help Jack. Borrow says that Jack is what he is and that he made the same mistakes all over again. He tells Jack to face the future. Jack returns to Regina blaming her for his troubles. He strangles her as the police knock on his door.

This was Leslie Nielsen's fourth appearance on *Tales of Tomorrow.* He would star on one more episode, "Ghost Writer."

Jack Gould of *The New York Times* didn't much like this episode. After it aired, he wrote:

As for "Tales of Tomorrow," its presentation on Friday was an item of indescribable trash and totally bereft of any dramatic worth. For its climax there was shown the gruesome choking to death of a girl. Then her lifeless feet and legs were dragged around the room as the camera came in for a sustained close-up. The scene was thoroughly unpleasant.

The newly merged A.B.C.-United Paramount network should not only worry about getting new shows. A little housecleaning would seem to be in order.[30]

"The Great Silence" – February 20, 1953

Cast: Burgess Meredith
Lila Skala
Paul Ford
Charles McClelland
William Kemp
Glenn Styres
Writer: Frank De Felitta
Director: Don Medford

The alien from "The Great Silence."

"The Great Silence" was unique in that most of the episode was done without spoken dialogue. People all over the United States are losing their ability to speak as a result of a hydrogen bomb test that is spreading a mist across the country that temporarily paralyzes the vocal cords.

Among those effected are a man and wife in the backwoods territory of a Western state. They are frustrated by not being able to communicate with each other. The wife wants her husband played by Burgess Meredith to go hunting for food. In the woods, he comes upon a space craft inhabited by an alien. The man attempts to inform his wife to no avail. He then goes to the town's municipal building to tell officials there. However, since he is illiterate, he cannot write down what he has seen. Returning home, he decides to dynamite the space craft. His wife comes upon the debris and her injured husband. Both of their voices return, and he says everything is all right now.

"The Lonesome Village" – February 27, 1953

Cast: Raymond Bailey
Heywood Hale Broun
Stephen Elliott
Buzz Martin
Natalie Priest
Constance Clausen
Writers: Jack Barden & Irwin Blacker
Director: Don Medford

According to the script for this installment, the camera opens: "... on a test tube rack set on a lab table in limbo. The test tubes are half filled. Suddenly, of their own accord, they burst and the liquid runs down the rack." The camera then "...dissolves onto a transparent world globe that is lighted from inside. The globe flickers and brightens briefly and then the light slowly dims. The ballad of the lonesome village is heard in the background against this picture."[31]

A singer performs the ballad that begins:

"A mutant life unreconciled---
An unseen killer in the night
Dispensing horror, death and blight,
A plague unleashed, a fury crazed,
Has struck the earth and left it dazed.
And just one village now survives,
Quite unaware, as dawn arrives."[32]

Ann Latham prepares to leave her husband because she is sick of the small town in which she lives with the townspeople not friendly to her since she is not a native of the village. She wants to go to a nearby city and resume her career as a nurse.

Will, her husband and the town's mayor, discovers that there is no electricity in their home and the phone is dead. Jake, a friend, stops by and says that many people have died in the nearby city and that he had been attacked by an axe-wielding man who subsequently died. He describes all the people who died in the city lying in the streets.

On a small portable radio, Will hears that a plague has struck with many deaths and the few people that are alive have gone mad. The entire world is affected. Apparently, the water in Will's small town has radioactive minerals that make the townspeople immune to the plague as long as they drink the water.

Other townspeople come to the Latham house asking about the plague. A twelve-year-old boy named Roger explains that his parents went to the city overnight and weren't planning to return until tonight. He believes they are dead. Jake informs Will that he checked the local grocery store and there should be enough food for the villagers for a while.

Ann tells Will that she realizes she is now trapped in the village. A man in the final stages of the mutant bacillus arrives at the Latham's. He stumbles and collapses. The man is Roger's father barely recognizable.

That evening, Will holds a meeting of the villagers to plan a course of action on rationing food and fuel. They discuss what to do if strangers show up in the village. One man wants to shoot them. One villager enters Will's house holding a gun on another man who was looting the local store for salt and matches.

A woman named Grace who had a physical encounter with Roger's now-deceased father thinks she has come down with the plague. Ann tells her that she is immune like everyone else in the village.

Jake brings Roger back who had run away to find his parents. Roger had been attacked by a city resident who had gone berserk. Ann takes care of Roger as the townsfolk rally around Ann because of her medical knowledge.

The episode ends with the singer finishing his ballad:

> "The stars glide on and skies grow clear.
> The earth revolves from year toward year.
> The village in the hills survives.
> The elder pass and youth arrives.
> Bacilli die—the lesson's learned,
> And men to farther hills returned.
> The stars look down and they are carin'
> For life goes on while men have carin'
> For life goes on while men have darin'
> And this is how the world will die—
> With one arm reaching toward the sky."[33]

Not only was this episode one that had an original song as part of the story but it also portrayed radioactivity in a positive light instead of causing the end of mankind as did several other *Tales of Tomorrow* presentations.

"The Fury of the Cocoon" – March 6, 1953

Cast: Peter Capell as Brenegan
Nancy Coleman as Susan
Cameron Prud'Homme as Borden
Fernande Gude as the guide
Writer: Frank De Felitta
Director: Don Medford

The plaster cast of a large insect from "The Fury of the Cocoon."

The story focused on scientists sent to investigate a meteorite that crashed into a site in the jungle. At their base camp, two of the scientists – Borden and Brenegan, find a large cocoon broken open. Later they discover one of their colleagues dead with his throat pierced and drained of blood. Borden and Brenegan subsequently find another member of the expedition named Susan, exhausted and incoherent. The deceased explorer's journal reveals that a meteorite brought invisible insects the size of large dogs to the jungle that feed on human blood. The deceased colleague was able to chloroform one of the insects that emerged from a cocoon and make a plaster cast of it. The creature had large eyes, teeth, and claw-like appendages.

Susan informs the other two explorers that there are hundreds of such insects around. Borden and Brenegan attempt to secure the base camp so the creatures do not break in while they are sleeping. The creatures begin scraping at the cabin at night. One enters and attacks Brenegan. With Susan's help, Borden ties it up with a rope. Later, Brenegan decides to take his chances and leave the cabin on his own. Naturally, he is killed by the insects. At daybreak, Susan and Borden flee to the river. Before leaving, they discover that the insect they had tied up is now dead from insecticide in the cabin. They take cans of insecticide with them spraying the contents behind them as they travel to the river to escape.

Writer De Felitta attempted to launch a speculative fiction TV series of his own called *Witchcraft* to be hosted by Franchot Tone and produced by Charles H. Norton.

In November 1953, Tone signed an agreement with Charles H. Norton to host this weekly thirty-minute anthology based on the works of William Seabrook. The series would relate stories of the supernatural and paranormal activity. The pilot was produced in 1954.

In the opening, Tone, on a set designed to be Seabrook's study, introduced the pilot episode titled "The Doll in the Brambles." Louis, a Frenchman, is about to marry Marie (Annemarie Roussel). His friend Fred Hunter (Darrin McGavin) arrives in France from the United States to attend the wedding. Louis informs him that the wedding is canceled because Marie's step grandmother Madame Tirelou (Blanka Yurka), a witch, forbids Marie from ever seeing Louis again. When Madame Tirelou sees Marie and Louis together in the woods, she places a wooden doll that looks like Louis in some brambles. Subsequently, Louis is caught in brambles and finds that his legs are paralyzed. The doctor who examines Louis believes that the paralysis is psychosomatic. After Fred removes the doll from the brambles, Louis recovers. He and Fred rescue Marie before her step grandmother casts a spell on her. Fred approaches Madame Tirelou as she recites incantations, and the old woman falls to her death when backed onto a balcony that is in disrepair.

The pilot was never turned into a television series.

"Squeeze Play" – March 13, 1953

Cast: John McQuade
Joseph Wiseman
Elizabeth York
Murvyn C. Vye
Robert Patten
Charlotte Knight
Writer: Mann Rubin
Director: Don Medford

Randy Shane is a reporter for the *Star Chronicle* in this episode which opens with the editor of the newspaper, Art Trowler, working on an editorial for the morning edition. Shane bursts into Trowler's office looking disheveled. Trowler says that he doesn't know Shane even though Shane says that they have been colleagues for over ten years. When Trowler threatens to call the police, Shane pulls a gun on him. He asks Trowler to concentrate on his face to try to remember him. Shane says he won a Pulitzer Prize for the paper in 1947. Trowler replies that Ed Gold won that prize. Shane says that Gold is a name planted in Trowler's brain so that the editor forgot about Shane.

Randy Shane asks Trowler to recall a hypnotist named Waldo, the Mental Marvel. Trowler had tasked Shane with doing a series of articles about the hypnotist. Shane talks about taking a girl named Nedra, to whom Waldo was engaged, away from the hypnotist. Shane wrote a series of articles about the European hypnotist appearing in America. Waldo blamed Shane for Nedra's suicide saying that she was depressed when Shane left her. Randy Shane told Waldo that the hypnotist was a fraud. The hypnotist responded that he has a new weapon to fight Shane. Shane said that Nedra always hated Waldo and wanted to get as far away from him as possible. Shane planned to tell the world in his articles that Waldo is a fraud.

At his boarding house, Shane's female acquaintance, Bonnie Vickers, reads his first article about the hypnotist. Waldo visits Shane to complain about the article and demands a retraction. Waldo says that his bookings are being canceled because of the newspaper report. Shane asks the hypnotist to leave. Waldo threatens to use hypnosis to make people forget whole fragments of their lives.

Randy Shane's second story about Waldo references the fact that the hypnotist collaborated with the Nazis during the second World War. After his third story is published, when Shane returns to his boarding house, neither his landlady nor Bonnie Vickers recognize him. They think he is crazy.

Trowler doesn't believe Shane's story even though Shane insists that Waldo's use of mass hypnosis is why no one remembers him. He goes on to tell Trowler that, after he left the boarding house, he went to see Waldo. Waldo told him that he didn't recognize Shane and that he is leaving America for Europe. Continuing to relay his story to Trowler, Shane says that all his friends no longer remember him and that he is fading out of existence – gradually disappearing and being squeezed out of life. Trowler asks Shane to come back the next morning after he has some rest. As Shane leaves, a young reporter brushes by him almost knocking him over. Trowler tells the reporter about the crazy story he just heard. The reporter responds that there was no one there other than Trowler when he entered the office – that Trowler was all alone.

Mann Rubin wrote ten episodes of the series – more than any other writer. He also adapted stories written by others for *Tales of Tomorrow*. Rubin, born in 1927, earned his bachelor's degree from New York University and became a science fiction writer for *Strange Adventures* and *Mystery in Space*. He subsequently had his short stories published in the *Alfred Hitchcock* magazine. He passed away in 2013 at age eighty-six.

"Read to Me, Herr Doktor" – March 20, 1953

Cast: Mercedes McCambridge as Patricia
Everett Sloane as Professor Kimworth
William Kemp as Sidney
Ernest Graves as the voice
Writer: Alvin Sapinsley
Director: Don Medford

The amateurish appearance of the Herr Doktor, robot.

Professor Kimworth, with failing eyesight, has created a robot, Herr Doktor, that reads to him. A former student of the professor's wants to market the concept, but Pat, the professor's daughter, dislikes the creation, particularly as it takes on more human characteristics. The robot begins talking not only to the professor but also to Pat as it begins walking and telling the professor and his daughter what to do. The robot develops a love for learning and wants to take on full human traits.

Herr Doktor has the professor begin teaching it by asking the professor to read to it. The robot warns Pat against seeking outside help or else it will end her father's life. When the professor has taught the robot everything he knows, it seeks to romance Pat. Herr Doktor accuses the professor of coming between it and Pat. She says it will never have her love and that the books her father read to his creation about fighting for the love of a woman are all wrong about real love. Hearing this, the heart of the machine breaks, and the robot "dies."

Writer Alvin Sapinsley later scripted episodes for series like *The Untouchables*, *The Virginian*, and *Kojak*. For a time in the 1950's, he was blacklisted for having attended Communist Party meetings.

"Ghost Writer" – March 27, 1953

Cast: Leslie Nielsen as Bert
Gaby Rodgers as Joan
Murray Matheson as Lee Morton
Harry Mehaffey as Lou
Writer: Mann Rubin
Director: Don Medford

Leslie Nielsen starred in more episodes of *Tales of Tomorrow* than any other actor. He was also featured in several other anthologies of the 1950s including *Kraft Theatre, Studio One*, and *Playhouse 90* and transitioned to primarily comedy roles later in his career in the series *Police Squad* and the films *Airplane, Naked Gun* and several others up until his death in 2010.

"Ghost Writer" told the story of Bert, a struggling writer working on his first novel. He receives a letter from Lee Morton about working for him on a part-time basis to complete stories Morton has started but has been unable to complete. Morton agrees to pay Bert $500 for each story he finishes. He completes one and then does two others.

The next day, after reading the newspaper, Bert finds that the first story for which he wrote the ending actually happened. It involved the death of a night club singer murdered by another man who, in turn, was strangled by a second man.

The next story also comes true with a hotel burning to the ground. Bert's wife Joan tells him that she checked with the Writer's Guild about Morton and the organization said they never heard of him. Joan threatens to leave Bert if he collaborates any more with Morton. He goes to Morton's home to return the money he was paid and explains why he cannot work for the man anymore. Morton wants Bert to do one final story for which he will receive $1000. It is about someone running away from an impossible situation and a woman being killed in a taxi cab accident. Bert decides to take the final assignment for the money. His wife calls Morton and learns what Bert has done. Bert leaves to see his wife who has left her job and taken a cab. He runs after her, but it is too late. The accident takes place, and his wife dies.

This episode was another original script by Mann Rubin. After *Tales of Tomorrow* was canceled, Rubin wrote a short story, "The Second Voice" published in the March 1954 issue of *Fantastic Universe* that could have been the basis for a *Tales of Tomorrow* presentation.

The story focused on Robbie Crawford, a ventriloquist, who, with his dummy Spud, is appearing at Harlow Field in a show for the troops. Harlow Field is the largest experimental base in the world, the proving ground for top secret military weapons. Two months out of every year, Crawford devotes time to travel the USO circuit.

Before his scheduled show, Colonel Meadows, the Commanding Officer of Harlow Field, and another man visit Crawford. The other man is identified as Dr. Paul Shalt, who specializes in the development of radar, at the base.

During Crawford's rehearsal with Spud, Shalt had been testing, in different areas of the auditorium, Crawford's "second voice" – the one he uses for his dummy. That voice is perfect for Shalt's experiment. The physicist wants to use the second voice for an experiment that will transmit the voice to Mars. As the doctor explains, a voice in the higher octave like Crawford uses for Spud has a certain resonant intonation which can be curved and regulated in any direction. Since Mars is now the closest to earth, the experiment must take place immediately.

The experiment will take fifteen minutes for the voice to reach Mars and fifteen minutes for its return. Those regulating the voice in the control room will hear nothing but vibrations during the initial transmission. Only on its return to earth will the voice be audible.

Crawford and Spud are ushered into a soundproof room to begin the transmission. Dr. Shalt and Colonel Meadows watch but cannot hear what Crawford is saying. After a period of time, they hear Spud's voice coming back from Mars with Spud saying that his voice is being sent by a newly invented Amplification Unit and extending greetings to the beings on Mars. A commanding, authoritative voice from Mars responds to the message, stating that Mars does not like intruders. The message ends with the warning to stay away and not wanting any further contact from earth.

Meadows and Shalt think that Crawford was playing a trick on them imitating a voice from Mars. Crawford denies that he is the voice from Mars. Meadows and Shalt believe that Crawford has been working too much and maybe forgot what he said on the transmission, but the ventriloquist denies ever saying that no further contact with Mars should be made.

In any event, Crawford must leave to go to the auditorium for his show. An army announcer is there to engage Crawford in conversation with Spud. When Crawford tries to speak through Spud, only a gurgle comes out of Spud's mouth. The mouth of the dummy flaps open and shut without any sound emanating. Crawford screams that he has lost his voice. The Martians stole his voice.

Colonel Meadows tells the audience about the experiment in which Crawford had participated and that the ventriloquist had suffered a temporary shock on hearing his voice return from the Red Planet. He assures the audience that Crawford will receive the best medical care. A guest vocalist appears, and the show continues.

"Past Tense" – April 3, 1953

Cast: Boris Karloff as Dr. Henry Marco
Robert F. Simon as Giles

Katherine Meskill as Jan
John McGovern as Laskey
Allen Nourse as Bonzy
Writers: Jack Weinstock & Willie Gilbert based on an idea by Robert F. Levine, ad agency executive
Director: Don Medford

In 1953, Dr. Henry Marco invents a time machine in his laboratory. He is tired of being poor and treating his patients for routine ailments. His wife, Jan, wants to destroy the time machine so he will return to his regular medical practice. Nevertheless, he insists on going back to the past to introduce the drug penicillin and become wealthy when drug companies start manufacturing it.

Initially, Marco goes back to 1923 to show executives at one drug company the uses of penicillin. He demands $250,000 for information about the drug. But the head of the company, Dr. Giles, will not grant permission to use the drug on patients. Another doctor at the firm, Dr. Laskey, does allow Marco to treat a patient who is severely ill with pneumonia. Because the woman is too sick for the drug to be effective, she dies. Laskey is fired. Marco tries to explain that the patient was beyond all help, but the company will not permit further experimentation.

Marco returns to the 1950's and tells his wife that he is going back to 1910 to try to sell penicillin to the same drug company. He meets again with Laskey and Giles but comes up against the same resistance to using the drug. Marco comes down with pneumonia and, in his hospital bed, he keeps saying the word "penicillin" as he succumbs.

The writers of this installment, Jack Weinstock and Willie Gilbert, also scripted episodes of other early science fiction series like *Tom Corbett, Space Cadet, Captain Video and His Video Rangers,* and *Rod Brown of the Rocket Rangers.*

"Homecoming"- April 10, 1953

Cast: Edith Fellows
Brian Keith
Doro Merande
Harry Shepard
Johnny Olsen as Bill Compton
Al Checo
Story: Ray Bradbury
Adapter: Mann Rubin
Director: Don Medford

Two years earlier, an Air Force plane carrying Andy Willis crashed in the Arctic. Now, Bill Compton, a newscaster, reports live from the Willis household on the day of Andy Willis' homecoming. Sarah Willis, Andy's mother, shows the interviewer a portrait of Andy. Sam Willis reminisces about his son's accomplishments, showing off a full trophy case. The interviews are interrupted by an update that Andy has landed. The radio announcer approaches Andy who is glad to be back but begins coughing mysteriously. Back in the Willis household, Bill Compton interviews Andy's wife, Norma Willis. She recalls how they met in the sixth grade and were married only a year before Andy's disappearance. The family's interviews end as sirens announce Andy's return home.

Andy Willis is invisible as he enters. His briefcase floats mid-air, and the camera crew is confused. His family does not seem to react to Andy's invisibility as they welcome him home. Bill Compton and the rest of the news crew check their equipment, unsure of why the cameras can't see him. Meanwhile, Andy surreptitiously informs Norma that he has something important to tell her. Something within his body has changed, and he no longer functions like a normal human. He mentions weapons testing, gamma rays, and his downed plane. Sarah Willis brings in tea, sending Andy into a panic as he knocks the tray away. The tea is too hot. Andy reacts as if pained by the steam.

The news team confirms that there is nothing wrong with their equipment. They do, however, find a strange trail of ice chips outside. Andy excuses himself to speak to Norma in another room. The perspective shifts to first-person from Andy's point of view. He explains that his body is deteriorating quickly and that the ice chips came from him. When his plane was downed in the Arctic, Andy was exposed to sub-zero temperatures without protection, yet couldn't feel the cold. He will not survive in this warmer climate, but has returned to say his goodbyes. Norma wants to go back to the Arctic with him, but Andy refuses. They share a kiss.

Sarah goes to check on Andy and Norma, but finds that Andy is gone. He has left a letter, which she reads aloud. Andy is afraid that his radiation exposure could infect others, and has escaped to the Arctic to both survive and prevent others from sharing his fate. Norma doubts that the radiation could be transmissible. The camera crew pans to her seated, invisible, on a rocking chair.

Mann Rubin adapted this story from "Homecoming," a tale by Ray Bradbury that was about a person who was a misfit. Aunts, uncles, cousins, grandparents, and other relatives are all arriving at the home where young Cecy and her brother Timothy live. They are all coming to celebrate Allhallows Eve.

Timothy awakens at sunset and washes his face in front of the only mirror in the house. He can't get used to the routine of sleeping during the day and being awake all night. Unlike the rest of his family, his teeth are malformed. They are weak, and he doesn't have incisor-like steel spikes. In addition, he is afraid of the dark and has no wings sprouting from his shoulder blades. Timothy prays to the "Dark One" to help him grow up and be like his siblings.

The entire extended family arrives at midnight. His sister Laura says that her brothers, who work at a funeral home, provide sustenance for the whole family except for Timothy who doesn't like blood. His Uncle Einar throws Timothy into the air trying to make him fly.

At sunrise, most of the relatives go to the cellar to sleep in their mahogany boxes. Upstairs, Timothy tells Cecy that he wants to do something at the party to make his relatives pay attention to him, to make himself feel that he belongs. With Cecy's spirit inside of him and in front of everyone, he drinks a glass of warm red liquid. He then leaps from the top of the stairs but the wings he thought he had dissolve on the way down. His Uncle Einar catches him.

The uncle tries to comfort him. His mother says that they all love him no matter how different from the others he is.

Perhaps because *Tales of Tomorrow* did not ordinarily focus on stories of speculative fiction dealing with fantasy and the supernatural, Rubin turned the Bradbury story from fantasy to a science fiction yarn.

Ray Bradbury's stories became the basis for several episodes of TV anthologies including an episode of *The Twilight Zone* – "I Sing the Body Electric." He is, of course, most remembered for *Fahrenheit 451*, *The Martian Chronicles*, and *The Illustrated Man.*

Mann Rubin had a final venture into speculative fiction in a 1973 installment of the William Castle anthology, *Circle of Fear*, starring then husband and wife, John Astin and Patty Duke Astin as spouses.

In "Graveyard Shift," John Astin appeared as Fred Colby, a former actor for Fillmore Studios who is now a security guard at the establishment. His wife Linda is pregnant.

Fillmore Studio is closed and due to be demolished. When Fred goes on duty for the night shift, he is warned that a gang of teens has been causing mischief around the studio lot. Fred hears voices and goes to investigate but can't locate the source. He enters a studio projection room which is showing an old horror movie made by the studio but cannot find anyone in the room.

When his shift ends, he goes home to his wife. While trying to sleep, Fred hears voices again but this time finds they are coming from a movie Linda is watching on television. That night, he returns to work. The gang of teens sneaks back to the movie lot, dress up in costumes from the wardrobe building, and start making noise. Fred hears a voice welcoming him back to the studio. His wife comes by to give him a snack while he is working. He hears a crash and runs to force the gang of teenagers off the lot. Meanwhile, his wife hears voices calling her name. She follows the voices to a soundstage and sees various characters from old horror movies asking her to choose one of them. Fred responds to her screams, and the visions disappear.

Linda asks Fred to get a new job as a used car salesman offered by her uncle. When he visits the uncle about the job offer, on a radio in one of the cars, Fred hears the same voices telling him to come back. They need Fred to save them.

The following day, Fred returns to his job as a security guard and hears the voice of a director and sees visions of a crew making a film. He is almost killed when a lighting fixture from the ceiling falls near him.

Fillmore, the former head of the studio comes by one night to look around one last time. He discusses *Dr. Death*, an unsuccessful film the studio had made. The main character, in league with the devil, would take over the minds of others. Fred believes that the Dr. Death character is terrorizing him and his wife. He abruptly leaves and goes home to his wife. He finds his wife frightened by characters from the *Dr. Death* film. He shoots at them. A doctor comes by recommending that Linda be hospitalized. Fred explains to Linda that the old movie characters want to live on after the studio is demolished. Linda theorizes that one of the characters wants to be chosen by her to possess her baby.

Fred returns to the studio, but the new guard informs him that he has been fired. He pleads to be left in one last time to gather his belongings. Knocking out the guard, Fred sets fire to the canisters of old film. The voices yell for help but eventually cease. Fred returns to the hospital to find that Linda has delivered a healthy baby boy.

"The Rival" – April 17, 1953

Cast: Anthony Ross
Mary Sinclair
Story: Stephen French Whitman
Adapter: James P. Cavanagh

An older man weds a young woman who finds that, after she moves into his home, she has a rival for his affection – his pet cat.

According to IMDb, this episode was based on the story by Stephen French Whitman titled "The Rival." The short story concerned a man named Nicholas Tyndale whose hobby is the occult. Laura Della Fagginola is in love with Tyndale. She is also a medium who can contact the spirit world. Laura has been holding seances for Nicholas. He has her conjure up a formidable rival for his affection. The rival appears as a living woman slightly blurred as if seen through an aura of vapor. In the end, Nicholas is so enamored of her that he commits suicide when her vision disappears.

"Please Omit Flowers"- April 24, 1953

Cast: Ann Burr
Frank Albertson
Writer: James Blumgarten

A mortician develops a serum that induces a deep sleep resembling death. He finds he can increase his business with people who want to fake their own death and begin a new life somewhere else.

James Blumgarten scripted episodes of the DuMont Network Television series, *The Stranger*, about a man who mysteriously appears to aid people in their fight for justice. In addition, he authored the science fiction novel, *The Astronaut*, about a man who rockets into space and then mysteriously disappears.

"The Evil Within" – May 1, 1953

Cast: James Dean as Ralph
Margaret Phillips as Anne Crane
Rod Steiger as Peter Crane
Writer: Manya Starr
Director: Don Medford

Peter Crane brings home a box containing an experimental serum that he developed. It needs to be refrigerated, and the refrigerator at his lab is not working. The serum makes animals lose their inhibitions. His wife, Anne, dislikes the fact that her husband neglects her and focuses too much on his work. He tells her that he needs to develop an antidote to the effects of the serum.

While her husband takes a walk, Anne finds that some of the serum has dripped from a test tube onto a pie she has in the refrigerator. She eats some of the pie and begins feeling strange adopting a sexy persona. Ralph, her husband's lab assistant, calls to leave a message for Peter, but Anne refuses to take a message. She rips up her husband's notes containing the serum's formula and sets them on fire. She also pours the remainder of the serum down the kitchen sink.

The next day, Peter finds the serum missing. Anne, all dolled up in a black negligee and make-up, says that she accidentally knocked it over and threw it away. He says he can make more but then finds that the formula is missing. Anne tells him that he left his notebook at the lab and that Ralph never left him a message.

At the lab, Peter doesn't find the notebook. He attempts to replicate the serum from memory but fails. Ralph says that he did call Anne the night before. When Peter returns home early from work, his wife thinks that it means he will pay more attention to her. Peter questions his wife about what happened the previous night. She says that Ralph did call and said terrible things about her husband and admits that she burned the notebook. He opens the refrigerator and finds some of the serum on the pie. He explains that he will develop the antidote to counteract the effects of the serum so his wife can be herself again. Anne picks up a big knife threatening to kill herself. In reaction, Peter says that he will give up his career if she puts down the knife.

Ralph phones saying that the animals who were given the serum are now normal after twenty-five hours and thirty minutes. Peter asks Anne to give him fifteen minutes to tell her all the things that he has wanted to say to her thinking that after that time, she will return to her old self. The times passes. She drops the knife, and they embrace.

This was one of several early television appearances by James Dean before he achieved movie stardom.

Writer Manya Starr is probably best remembered for her work on various daytime dramas such as *First Love*, *The Clear Horizon*, and *Paradise Bay*.

"The Vault" – May 8, 1953

Cast: Dorothy Peterson
Cameron Prud'Homme
Helen Auerbach
Liam Sullivan
Writer: David Karp
Director: Unknown

While doing scientific tests deep within the earth's core, four people find themselves trapped believing that a nuclear war has occurred on earth. They wonder if they are the only humans left.

David Karp, who scripted this episode, went on to write novels and several other scripts for television series including *The Untouchables* and *The Defenders.*

"Ink" – May 15, 1953

Cast: Joseph Anthony
Mildred Natwick
Katherine Balfour
Writer: Frank De Felitta
Director: Don Medford

In a lush home library, Leland and Ann embrace for a kiss. They part, and Leland shows off an expensive book the college recently acquired. It is a book of spells. Ann reads a snippet aloud. Leland proposes, but the proposal sets off an argument. Ann refuses the proposal because of Belle, Leland's sister. Belle raised Leland and seems to despise Ann. They speculate that it might be academic jealously, as both women work in the chemistry department at the college. Ann shares news that she has completed the manuscript for her textbook and was even offered a permanent position as head of the chemistry department. She turned the job down, suggesting that Belle deserves the position more than she does. Ann leaves the room.

Leland returns to the book of spells and reads a spell about an ink that compels all that read it to obey its commands. Belle bursts in the door and announces her new position as head of the chemistry department. They chat, but the excitement is broken when Leland tells Belle that he has proposed to Ann. Belle is deeply upset.

Insulted by Belle's unfavorable opinions about Ann, Leland retorts that Ann is why Belle even got her new position. Leland leaves in a huff. Alone, Belle wanders to the spell book.

As she reads, her body suddenly goes stiff. She marches to the fireplace, takes a poker, and smashes the mirror hanging over the mantle. The spell book is shown, with a page reading "Destroy all reflections before you." Belle tears the page out and takes it to her laboratory. She scrapes ink from the page into a beaker, reconstitutes the ink, and pours it into an inkwell.

The following morning, Belle and Leland engage in a new argument about Ann. Leland declares that they will be married whether Belle likes it or not and storms away. Furious, Belle pens a letter to Ann using the magic ink.

Meanwhile, Ann tells Leland she plans to leave. He begs her to stay, but she only asks him to check the mail for a letter from her textbook publisher. No letter has arrived yet, either from Belle or the publisher. Later that day, Leland returns to tell Belle that Ann has turned down his proposal again. Ann respects Belle's feelings and does not want to cause further stress. Ann calls to check on the mail. Leland has a letter addressed to Ann, and assumes it is from the publisher. Belle tries desperately to get the letter away from him, chasing him. Ann lets herself in and takes her letter. Belle begs Ann not to open the letter, revealing that Ann will die if she reads it. Stunned, Ann hands the envelope over, and she and Leland leave.

Now alone, Belle takes the envelope back to her lab. She unfolds the letter, and it reads, "Destroy this letter, and then yourself." She stiffens the same way she did earlier. Belle burns the letter over her Bunsen burner, then walks offscreen to the window. The episode closes on a shot of an open window, its curtains billowing in the wind.

"The Spider's Web" – May 22, 1953

Cast: Nancy Coleman as Jean Crawford
Henry Jones as Irwin Crawford
Don Hanmer as Matt Radigan
Writer: Frank De Felitta
Director: Don Medford

On a deserted island in the Pacific, Matt Radigan along with Jean and Irwin Crawford wash ashore on a life raft. Jean is seeking a divorce from Irwin. Irwin explores the island finding exotic giant insects thinking they are mutations produced by atomic radiation. The group sees a sign that atomic refuse has been buried on the island.

Irwin encounters a nest of large spider eggs and then sees a giant spider's web that must have been spun by a mammoth arachnoid. The Crawford's want to get away, but Radigan says that they should stay in the clearing where the web is since darkness will soon come. They rig up a rope and canvas to trap the spider. When the spider comes into the trap, Radigan shoots it.

That night, as Radigan and Jean sleep, Irwin takes Radigan's gun, leaves a message about survival, and goes off. Discovering that Irwin has left, Jean and Radigan go to find the life raft leaving Jean's husband alone on the island to fend off the other giant spiders that pursue him as he becomes stuck in a large web.

This episode appears to be another original work by Frank De Felitta while engaged in his "monster" phase for *Tales of Tomorrow* (e.g., "The Fatal Flower," "The Cocoon," "The Fury of the Cocoon"). Some sources indicate that this episode was derived from a short story by Henry Christopher Bailey called "The Spider's Web," but that is not correct.[34] The Bailey story involves the disappearance of a judge whom some felt was soft on crime in which a spider web is a clue to solving the mystery. The story had nothing to do with a large spider produced by atomic radiation.

"Lazarus Walks" May 29, 1953

Cast: Olive Deering
William Prince
Joseph Wiseman
Story: Peggy Speed
Adapter: James P. Cavanagh

The episode for this *Tales of Tomorrow* entry appears to have been lost. However, the story was first presented on the radio version of the series *Suspense* in the 1940s.

Based on the radio episode, the story concerned Robert Graham, a doctor of psychiatry, who lives in a big house with his wife Isabel, a concert pianist, and her aunt Jane. Isabel is having problems with her nerves and no longer performs in public while the doctor cares for her.

One day, Roger Holcomb phones the doctor for an appointment. Holcomb had been brought back from the dead after being clinically dead for four minutes. He has developed a strange condition from the experience. He can tell when a person is lying and has a compulsion to tell the liar the truth. He is now shunned by everyone he knows. Dr. Graham invites him to stay at his house while the doctor studies him and hopefully cures him. The doctor tells Holcomb that he – the doctor, inherited a fortune. Holcomb responds with the truth that it is really Isabel who inherited the fortune.

Aunt Jane believes that Graham is using his wife's sickness to keep her fortune. The aunt tells Isabel that she should leave her husband. When the doctor and Holcomb enter the room, Holcomb blurts out that the aunt has been telling her niece to leave the doctor. Jane decides to no longer stay with her niece and husband.

Isabel begins losing her friends because of Holcomb's truth-telling. She wants to return to the concert stage. A concert master is coming for dinner to discuss her comeback, and Isabel doesn't want

Holcomb at the meal. Holcomb says that death will prevent Isabel from ever playing again.

Later, Isabel goes to talk with Holcomb in his room. She says that her husband is interfering in the relationship between Holcomb and her. She believes that Holcomb is cured of his habit of telling the truth when he hears a lie.

The doctor interrupts the meeting and asks Isabel to give Roger Holcomb a shot to calm him. Isabel leaves the room after administering the injection. She sees Holcomb again. The doctor goes to Holcomb's room and finds him dead with a hypodermic needle beside him. He thinks that Isabel killed Holcomb and calls the police. The police find Isabel's fingerprints on the hypodermic and conclude that she murdered Roger Holcomb. The doctor says that he never loved Isabel and just wanted her money. After Holcomb died, the doctor apparently inherited Holcomb's habit of telling the truth.

"What Dreams May Come" – June 12, 1953

Cast: Arnold Moss
Sally Gracie
Ernest Graves
Story: Walter de la Mare
Adapter: Kenneth White
Director: Unknown

Supposedly, this final episode of *Tales of Tomorrow* was based on a short story by Walter de la Mare. In the story, Emmeline wakes up in the back seat of a motor coach. She cannot remember where she came from or where she is going. She looks in her handbag and finds a scrap of paper from an envelope, but she is unable to decipher the address on it.

She asks the bus to stop and gets out. Emmeline begins walking toward some high iron gates and proceeds toward a large house. A man opens the door. She says that she is not sure where she is and gives the man the piece of paper. He replies that this is the place whose address is on the paper. The man shows her to a room and says the master will be there shortly. Emmeline thinks that she must leave before the master arrives, but she doesn't have the strength to do so. She stares at a portrait in the room which she assumes is of the master of the house. She recognizes his face. The inscription underneath the portrait reads: "All hope abandon ye who enter here!"

Emmeline then encounters a young nurse who tells her that she has nothing to be afraid of. Emmeline feels a bandage on her head. She falls asleep again; "… not even the most vigilant and skilful of nurses can keep a chart of her patient's dreams!"[35]

The *Tales of Tomorrow* episode did share the theme of recurring dreams with this short story. The television presentation concerned a wealthy young widow who marries her first love and former fiancé after the death of her husband. She becomes obsessed by dreams of her impending murder.

Unproduced Stories for *Tales of Tomorrow*

Early in the series run, two stories by Ray Bradbury were considered for the series but never produced.

Noted science fiction author Ray Bradbury's short stories not only inspired episodes of *Tales of Tomorrow* and *The Twilight Zone* but also many of them served as the basis for installments of his own anthology, *The Ray Bradbury Theater* which ran from 1985 to 1992.

One was "Zero Hour," in which seven-year-old Mink tells her mother that she is participating in a game called "Invasion." Only children less than ten-years old can play. Mink eats her lunch quickly so she can go back to the game. She knows that a new boy in town, Drill, is waiting for her. Drill is from another planet. Extraterrestrials couldn't figure out a way to attack earth. They needed help from earthlings and so enlisted impressionable children in their attempt at an invasion. Drill has told all kids that, after the invasion, they won't have to take baths and they can stay up late. Because older kids are making fun of the younger ones, the young kids say they will kill the older ones first.

Mink's mother receives a phone call from a friend who informs her that her kids are playing the same game. Her son tells her about Drill as well. They are saying that 5 o'clock is zero hour.

Mink's father comes home from work. Mink's mother hears a buzzing sound outside and then explosions occur all over the neighborhood. She and her husband take to the attic and hide there. She wants her husband to be quiet. They hear loud footsteps in the house. Fifty people crowd into their home with Mink calling out asking where her parents are. The attic door lock melts. The door opens. Mink peers inside with tall blue shadows behind her and says "Peekaboo."

The anthology series *Lights Out* aired an episode based on the story in July 1951 before *Tales of Tomorrow* premiered.

The other never-produced Bradbury story was "Marionettes, Inc." According to producer George Foley, "…there was no way to make the audience believe they were watching marionettes and we had to throw out the script."[36] The story was later adapted for an episode of *Alfred Hitchcock Presents.*

The November 9, 1958 presentation of the Alfred Hitchcock anthology, "Design for Loving" was based on "Marionettes, Inc." Set in 1965 America, Marian Seldes and Norman Lloyd starred as Lydia and Charlie Brailing. Charlie wants to re-energize his marriage by traveling the world; Lydia simply wants her husband to be more affectionate toward her.

That night, Charlie goes out drinking with a friend, Tom Smith (Elliott Reid), and shows him a ticket to Rio for one. Charlie has purchased a robot that looks and talks like him to be with his wife while he can enjoy time away from her. He uses a dog whistle to summon the robot when he wants it to leave his wife. He ordered the device from Marionettes, Inc. for $5000. The robot is kept in a large tool box in the basement when not in use.

Tom Smith thinks that he too will buy a robot to be with his wife when he wants to be away from her. Looking at his savings account, he is surprised to find that $5000 has been withdrawn recently for his spouse to buy a robot to replace her.

Charlie's robot begins to object to being placed in the large toolbox when not in use. Charlie threatens to send the robot back to the factory. The robot takes Charlie's plane ticket to Rio, puts Charlie in the tool box, and plans to go to Rio with Lydia.

Rod Serling, who created *The Twilight Zone,* wrote a script titled "The One-Eyed Man Is King" for an episode of *Tales of Tomorrow* that was never produced.

Dennis Carradine, a scientist, is jotting down notes when his friend, Bob Graves, a writer, stops by his laboratory. Bob asks Dennis where Mrs. Dill, the housekeeper, is. Dennis replies that he terminated her since he feels he doesn't really need a housekeeper. He goes on to say that she was much too curious about his experiments in time travel. He has constructed a special chair that supposedly transports people back in time. He tells Bob that he only wants to travel to the past since he feels he would be considered a wizard, a superman. If he were to travel to the future, he would probably be considered a barbarian, a lost soul. Dennis quotes the saying, "In the country of the blind, a one-eyed man is king."

Dennis wants to send his chair back in time and force someone to get into it and return to his present – 1953. He would then show the person all the technology of the present and what impresses the person the most, he would take back with him. In the seventeenth century, he plans to grow rich and powerful.

Bob leaves. Dennis uses the chair to transport a Pilgrim woman named Helen Osgood from Salem, Massachusetts to the present. He shows Helen around his living room demonstrating various items such as an electric lamp, a camera, a typewriter, and, outside, an automobile, etc. She reacts most strongly to a radio playing music. Bob comes by and is introduced to Helen.

When questioned by Bob about how she got a gold trinket she is wearing, Helen responds that she received it from a witch who was burned at the stake after she materialized in Salem. Her name was Agatha Dill – Dennis' housekeeper.

Bob castigates Dennis for what he did to Mrs. Dill. Dennis tells Bob that he will leave Helen in the present while he goes back to the year 1656. Dennis believes that he won't be burned at the stake. He intends to be the king of Salem. Dennis takes with him a pen, cigarette lighter, and a portable radio and materializes in Salem to the cries of "witch."

After claiming that he is not a witch, Dennis is asked by John, the leader of the townspeople, to demonstrate the items he has brought from the future. He shows everyone how the pen and the cigarette lighter work, but the radio doesn't broadcast anything since there are no radio transmissions in the seventeenth century. He tells the assembled group that he will go back and bring other twentieth century technologies to show them. A man throws a rock at Dennis injuring his eye. The crowd begins to destroy his time travel chair. John commands that a blind man be brought to face Dennis. John tells the scientist that the blind man will take care of him. Dennis is now a one-eyed king to the blind man.

Tales of Tomorrow: The Radio Series

The *Tales of Tomorrow* radio series adapted short stories from *Galaxy Science Fiction* magazine as the basis for its episodes. As with the television series, George Foley produced the radio show. Clark Andrews and Warren Sommerville directed the episodes which were adapted by Michael Sklar and Don Witty.

"Omentor," Raymond Edward Johnson, hosted each episode. The series aired from January 1, 1953 until April 9, 1953. It is often reported that the radio series moved to CBS beginning with its March 12, 1953 presentation. Nevertheless, newspaper listings at the time indicate the radio show continued on ABC until it ended in April 1953.

"Made to Measure" – January 1, 1953

Cast: Frank Baron as Joe
Helen Fields as Vera
Story: William Campbell Gault

No recording of the radio episode is available, but the short story, published in the January 1951 issue of *Galaxy* magazine, is as follows.

The story focuses on Joe, a scientist, working as Junior Assistant to the Adjutant Science Director, for an establishment at some time in the future. On a train ride home after work, Joe speaks with his friend, Sam Tullgren, the Director of the Domestic Center, about finding the perfect wife. He wants to create the perfect partner in the form of a robot. Joe has dealt with machines all his career, while Sam has dealt with people.

Joe is contemplating leaving his present wife Vera and replacing her with a more compatible mate. Vera begins packing to leave and go to the Domestic Center to find a new man. Joe wants a woman about 122 pounds in weight, and five feet, four inches tall with blonde hair and gray-green eyes. He has sketches and dimensions ready to build the robot.

Joe tells his boss what he is working on at home – a human but without human faults. He raises his voice to his boss and says that he thought his boss might be deaf as well as dumb. His boss threatens to fire Joe. Joe leaves work early.

He commences to work on his robot and names her Alice. He decides to show her off to the neighbors. Alice tells the neighbor's wife that she has surrendered to mediocrity. Joe has created a woman who is brutally honest and so decides to reprogram her to have more tact when dealing with people.

At work, Joe is instructed to meet with the Chief – his boss' boss about raising his voice to his boss. Joe makes out that it was all in jest and invites the Chief to dinner to meet his new partner. At dinner, the Chief relates a sad story about his late dog. Alice responds by saying "How touching," but she grins. The Chief asks why Alice can't frown. Joe works on her to make her frown as Alice becomes closer to being human.

Joe's friend Sam invites him and Alice over to play bridge. During the card game, Alice begins to lecture Sam's wife on the finer points of the game for one hour and nineteen minutes. Sam is relieved when Joe and Alice leave. Joe decides to make Alice less of a know-it-all.

Joe becomes disenchanted with his creation, desiring more of a human than a robot. He programs her to have a viewpoint of her own instead of sharing all the opinions that he has.

At work, Joe's boss wants to know more about Alice. Joe invites him to dinner. With her own opinions, Alice becomes infatuated with Joe's boss. She calls Joe egocentric, selfish, a humorless walking equation. Alice detests Joe. She wants a man like Joe's boss. Joe had made an image of himself, and it turned on him.

Joe now misses Vera and goes to the Domestic Center to find her. He tells her that he loves her and the two reconcile.

"The Biography Project" – January 8, 1953

Story: Dudley Dell (pseudonym for Horace L. Gold)

This short story was published in the September 1951 issue of *Galaxy* magazine. The radio presentation is apparently lost.

Arlington Prescott, a wiper in a contact-eye glass factory, invents a Biotime Camera that projects a temporal beam, reaccumulates it, and focuses it on a temporal-light-sensitized film. The camera can be used to photograph the past. A Biofilm Institute has been established based on Prescott's invention with one hundred Biotime Cameras. The Institute is a gift of Humboldt Maxwell, a wealthy manufacturer of Snack Capsules.

Teams of biographers, military analysts, historians, and others record history as it happens with special attention to past leaders of industry, politics, science, and the arts.

William Zatz, a Sunday supplement writer, focuses on mathematician Isaac Newton who, after making his observations on gravity, went on to investigate precognition, the philosopher's stone, and alchemy. Upon seeing the temporal beam, Newton thinks that someone is after his discoveries. A lip reader with the Institute interprets Newton's thoughts when he sees the mathematician's lips move.

Mowbray Glass, a psychiatrist with the Institute, opines that the Biotime Camera cannot be used anymore. Colleagues have been investigating the psychosis of German composer Robert Schumann, French novelist, Marcel Proust, and others who all eventually developed delusions of persecution because they believed they were being spied upon.

"Betelgeuse Bridge" – January 15, 1953

Cast: Lon Clark
John Gibson
John Stanley
Story: William Tenn (Phillip Klass)

This radio presentation concerned two intelligent aliens arriving in the United States. They land their space craft near Baltimore, Maryland. The aliens look like giant mollusks. A public relations man is enlisted to meet with them so that the aliens obtain a good impression of earth and its inhabitants. A documentary is made about the aliens who are dubbed Andy and Dandy. They appear to be very cooperative but reveal little about their planet and their intentions. Meanwhile, American scientists seek to determine the source of their space ship's power.

The aliens appear to be all things to all people. They go on live television for an interview where they reveal that they do not have a division of sexes like humans do. They also say they have machines called revitalizers which restore their cells periodically which is why they live five times longer than humans.

Appearing before the United Nations General Assembly, the head of the UN indicates that earthlings are interested in receiving a shipment of revitalizers. Humans will pay any price for such machines. The aliens confer with one another to determine what they would want in exchange for the machines. Ultimately they decide they would want earth's radioactive ore – all of it. Earthlings receive many revitalizers while all of earth's radioactive material is shipped to the alien's planet.

Humans begin using the revitalizers to extend their life spans. After six months, the revitalizers cease to work. The machines are found to be powered by uranium but now all of earth's uranium has been given to the aliens. The government decides to do a public relations campaign to prepare people for the truth about the revitalizers.

The story that inspired this episode was published in the April 1951 issue of *Galaxy Science Fiction*. Richard "Dick" Alvarez, a PR guy, is tasked with telling the public about the alien space craft and its two occupants. The aliens, looking like snails, have nine foot green trunks, pointed tops, and pink and white shells. They are from the planet Betelgeuse IX, ninth in line from the star named Betelgeuse. They are dubbed Andy and Dandy as in the radio episode or "Slugs with Superiority Complexes" because of their high intelligence although they portray themselves as deferring to humans. They provide evasive answers to questions like how long their trip to earth took and what they think about the democratic form of government.

To prepare the public for the revelation of the two aliens, a video is produced along with a comic strip featuring puppets that look like Andy and Dandy. Dolls for girls and small scooters for boys are manufactured with likenesses of the aliens. Becky Ann Joyce, a child star from Hollywood, is shown with the snails. A ticker tape parade is given them in New York City. The country goes wild over the two, and they embark on a world tour.

They appear on a TV show, *Celebrity Salon*, hosted by Bill Bancroft, who asks them if they are anxious to get home to their wives and children. Andy explains that they are hermaphrodites and have no family in the human sense. Bancroft also asks the two what ties they do have. Andy responds, "revitalizers," machines they expose themselves to every decade or so to stir up their cytoplasm and refresh themselves. The revitalizers extend their life expectancies.

Humans demand, as in the radio presentation, to have revitalizers so they can live for centuries instead of simply decades. Andy and Dandy will exchange revitalizers for earth's supply of radioactive minerals.

Large spaceships manned by small snail-like robots bring supplies of revitalizers to earth and take back all of earth's radioactive elements. Cancer, heart disease, kidney disease affecting humans disappear. However, six months after Andy and Dandy return to their planet, the revitalizers stop working. While the radio show ended there, the short story indicates that humans perfected artificial radiation and refueled the revitalizers. Alverez is then tasked with telling the aliens that the supply of radioactive material they received won't last forever and that, because humans developed artificial radioactive elements, earthlings want to resume trading with them.

"The Other Now" – January 22, 1953

Cast: Dick York as Jimmy Patterson
Lawson Zerbe as Hal Haynes
Story: Murray Leinster (Will F. Jenkins)

On the radio episode, Hal Haynes relates a story told to him by his friend, Jimmy Patterson. Coming home late at night from a party, Jimmy and his wife Jane are involved in an automobile accident where Jane loses her life.

One day, arriving home from work, Jimmy finds, in an ashtray, freshly smoked cigarette butts of the kind his wife used to smoke, but then the cigarette butts disappear. He questions if he really saw them or not. Later, he discovers his wife's diary on the top of a desk although he had locked it away in a trunk. Apparently, his late wife has made an entry on today's date writing about the car accident and commenting that she thought that her husband had died in the crash. But then the diary disappears.

Jimmy purchases a small camera to take photos of items that appear and disappear. He photographs the diary that has additional entries written by his wife. She wants to know where he is. Jimmy shows the photos to Hal who says that Jimmy has been seeing things, the photos are trick photography, and Jimmy has been writing diary entries in Jane's handwriting.

In response, Jimmy theorizes that there are multiple possible presents and futures and that Jane is in another dimension – an alternate reality.

A week goes by. Jimmy and Hal have dinner together when Jimmy says that he wants to be with his wife every night and that she is in an alternate reality. Time between the different realities begins to blur. Hal thinks that Jimmy should visit a psychiatrist.

Hal later talks with Jimmy over the phone. Jimmy says that he and Jane are very close and that Jane is coming through the time barrier. Hal visits Jimmy's apartment. No one answers the doorbell. Hal goes to the police, but they don't find anyone in the apartment. They cannot figure out how Jimmy left the apartment since everything is locked from inside.

The original story appeared in the March 1951 issue of *Galaxy Science Fiction*. The story is virtually identical to the radio play with Jimmy speculating, after a discussion with Hal, that there may be many alternate realities – one in which Jane has died, one in which Jimmy has died, one in which neither died, or one in which both had passed away.

The short story also makes it clear that Jimmy and Jane's accident occurred on a wet pavement when the truck carrying steel beams stopped quickly ahead of their car and one of the beams crashed through their car's windshield killing Jane.

"The Stars Are the Styx" – January 29, 1953

Cast: George Petrie
Story: Theodore Sturgeon

While a recording of the radio episode is not available, the short story is. "The Stars Are the Styx," published in the first issue of

Galaxy magazine (October 1950), focused on a man who is often referred to as Charon. The story begins:

> Every few years someone thinks to call me Charon. It never lasts. I guess I don't look the part. Charon, you'll remember, was the somber ferryman who steered the boat across the River Styx, taking the departed souls over to the Other Side. He's usually pictured as a grim, taciturn character, tall and gaunt.
>
> I get called Charon but that's not what I look like. I'm not exactly taciturn, and I don't go around in a flapping black cloak. I'm too fat. Maybe too old, too.[37]

The short story is relayed by the character of Charon who is really the Senior Release Officer at Curbstone. Curbstone, built 7800 years ago for heavy interplanetary transfers, is now the stepping off port to the rest of the universe. A young man named Judson arrives on Curbstone. He is an Outbounder. Flower, a so-so looking female also arrives along with a young male named Wold. Charon introduces Flower to Judson. Judson, Flower, and Wold are not yet certified to go out into the universe. Individuals who are certified can leave anytime they wish to go "Out," but, once they do, they can never return to Curbstone.

Charon shows Judson the ships that carry certified people out to the rest of the universe. The ships are like rooms with food lockers, air circulators, and synthesizers that convert energy to matter. The project of going Out to the rest of the universe lasts for 6000 years. Forty-six percent of Outbounders never get to where they are going. They become caught in a space-time nexus, die of old age because no one gets to them soon enough, or go mad and kill themselves. Judson confesses that he came to Curbstone because he is looking for something. Earth is under such strict discipline. Judson is searching either for something he lacks or for something he has not yet been able to identify.

The idea behind going Out is that the space ships that transport people are positioned in a great spherical pattern around space. They will send each other a blaze of tight-beam energy finding their neighbors and eventually earth.

Judson earns his certification to go Out and then marries Flower who is not yet certified. Wold also earns his certification.

Judson's marriage to Flower does not go well. He is killed by Wold because Wold is jealous of him marrying Flower whom Wold also liked. Charon finds Judson's body and catches Wold trying to dispose of it. Charon beats up Wold knocking him unconscious and places him in an Outbound ship with Judson's body.

"Syndrome Johnny" – February 5, 1953

Story: Charles Dye

The original story appeared in the July 1951 issue of *Galaxy Science Fiction* magazine. A donor's blood causes a syndrome consisting of endocrine imbalance, unique changes to appetite and digestion, and a general pattern of emotional disturbance in people who receive transfusions of the donor's blood.

After six years, people who had received blood transfusions spread the syndrome worldwide. The epidemic kills two out of every four people. For two subsequent years, the syndrome covered the world and then it disappeared leaving survivors with a tendency toward glandular problems. Later, a second epidemic occurred. Syndrome Johnny was the name given to the original blood donor.

A student of biochemistry theorizes that fetuses catch the syndrome in the womb and recover from it before being born. All newborns are carriers of the syndrome.

A police psychologist receives information that Syndrome Johnny may be in Peru and wants to investigate further. He goes to

Peru where he questions Dr. Ricardo Alcala about John Osborne Drake, also known as John Delogados, who works at Dr. Alcala's lab as a biochemist.

Alcala is currently researching the need for trace silicon in the human diet by ingesting silicon tablets himself. The doctor feels that he is turning into plastic.

The investigator tells Alcala that John Delogados may be Syndrome Johnny and that Johnny may be 140 years old. He has changed his name every twenty years. Dr. Alcala says that the Syndrome Plague is not a disease but an improvement in humans by making them stronger. Nevertheless, not all people have adjusted to the change which is why they need to ingest silicon. John Osborne Drake's father had been executed for unauthorized bacterial experiments that resulted in an epidemic and eight deaths.

Alcala shows the investigator how his skin has strengthened with the silicon tablets. It is now impervious to serious cuts and will not burn. Returning home, Alcala goes to see his friend, Johnny, and tells him that the Feds are after him. Johnny says that his work is now complete. He divulges that his father remade him chemically. A final plague will occur which will cement the chemical changes in humans. Johnny starts to leave. Dr. Alcala rushes after him and picks up a rock to hit Johnny. He drops the rock since his fist is enough like stone to crush a skull.

The radio version of the short story eliminated the background concerning how the syndrome was created and jumped right in to the investigation of Syndrome Johnny.

In the year 2090, at the headquarters of the Federated States of America, apparently an association of all the countries in North and South America, Lucius McVane, who heads the office of Health Control, is reading newspaper articles about Syndrome Johnny being found in Peru. He tasks Julio Camba, a special investigator for his department, to go to Peru to search for the man. Johnny is described as a solid-looking man with an unusual number of minor scars and a disturbing habit of cracking his fingers at the first-joint knuckles when he is thinking.

They have a thumbprint of the man taken from a hotel register. Lucius tells Julio that since there hasn't been a syndrome plague for thirty years, another one is about due since the man appears to be following a definite plan.

Meanwhile, in Peru, Dr. Ricardo Alcala is speaking with his wife Nita about another plague expected any time. They are worried about the effect of such an event on their daughter Alicia who is too frail to survive a plague. The doctor says that the previous plagues have opened up a whole new variety of diseases, most of them based on silicon deficiency, which he is researching.

Alcala goes to his lab where he speaks with another researcher named Del about his wife and daughter. He explains that his wife's mother had the syndrome but mostly recovered. His father also had it and recovered completely. But both he and his wife suffer from the after effects of the plague, and the effects have multiplied in their daughter. Del says that some people were able to adjust to the disease and become even healthier than before.

Julio goes to Peru to find syndrome Johnny. He talks with Dr. Alcala and asks if he knows John Osborne Drake otherwise known as John Delogados. The doctor lies to him saying Del is on a business trip and not available. At dinner, Alcala takes silicon tablets and reveals that all humans are turning into plastic since the plagues. His case is more advanced because he is taking the tablets. The doctor goes on to state that while his generation is still weak and ill from the shock of the change to their bodies and need silicon feeding, the illnesses mask the strength of his generation. Eventually, because of the plagues, humanity will be improved.

After dinner, Julio takes Alcala back to his lab. The doctor informs Del that the Feds are after him. Del explains to Alcala that his father built him into a carrier of the plague and says that his father saw the necessity of remaking the human race – making human bodies more durable. Furthermore, he indicates that his father thought that more than one plague would be necessary to complete his work, but Del says it is going to take four plagues to finish the work. He continues to theorize that those who survive the coming plague will be nearly perfect and that, one hundred years from now, there'll be little need for doctors on earth.

Del leaves. Dr. Alcala's wife appears and asks her husband if he is going to stop Del saying that with another plague, the living will not be able to bury the dead fast enough and that the doctor, her, and their daughter will die in the next plague.

The doctor then goes after Del telling him he can't start another plague. Del responds that the end justifies the means. The doctor threatens to kill him. Julio Camba appears to arrest Delogados. Del strikes Julio with a heavy blow murdering him. Del also says he will kill Dr. Alcala if he prevents him from escaping. The doctor replies that his fist from ingesting silicon is rock hard like Del's is. He strikes Del killing him and says that he developed his fist without starting a plague and that human perfection will have to wait.

"The Unimars Plot" – February 12, 1953

Not much is known about this radio episode. There is no story in the 1950, 1951, 1952, or early 1953 issues of *Galaxy* magazine with a title, "The Unimars Plot." The only information about this installment, found in newspapers at the time, is that the story is about "political agitation on Mars."

One possibility is that the episode is based on an original script. Another possibility is that the presentation was adapted from a short story by Isaac Asimov, "The Martian Way" that appeared in the November 1952 issue of *Galaxy* magazine.

"The Martian Way" concerns Mars and politics. It involves Ted Long, a Grounder from Mars, who is a mining engineer but becomes involved in space travel with his business partner, Mario

Esteban Rioz, a Martian Scavenger. They pilot a ship to retrieve space debris consisting of shells of booster rockets to reclaim the valuable metals of which the shells are made. When they capture such shells, they take them to Mars as salvage. Rioz has a friend, Richard Swenson, who co-pilots another scavenger ship. Because of the long space flights, each scavenger ship must have a pilot and a co-pilot.

On earth, a politician named Hilder is concerned that earth is not receiving anything from the salvaged shells, but Mars is dependent on earth for its water. The space ships of the era use water for propulsion.

A moratorium is placed on scavenging pending a decision from earth to enforce a more restrictive policy on sending water to Mars. Long, Rioz, and Swenson meet to discuss the feasibility of traveling far beyond Mars to capture millions of cubic miles of ice and bring it to Mars so that the planet is no longer dependent on earth for its water.

Back on earth, Hilder has mounted a campaign against "Wasters" - gangs of profit-seeking men using earth's resources for their own benefit. He has set up a committee to investigate waste in space flights. The choice for people on Mars is that they will have to either leave Mars and go to earth or else obtain water from somewhere else.

Rioz, Long, Swenson, and forty-seven other scavengers using twenty-five space ships travel to Saturn to obtain ice from one of that planet's rings. The space convoy is able to transport a gigantic chunk of ice from one of the planet's rings containing about a billion tons of water. The amount of water in the ice is about what earth would send Mars in over 200 years. When the convoy arrives on Mars, the planet's officials declare that they no longer need earth's water. Moreover, they are willing to send some of their water to earth if it needs the resource.

"Watch Bird" – February 19, 1953

Story: Robert Sheckley
According to the radio play, in the year 2003, the President of the United States orders watch birds be launched to cover every town in the country. The X2 model of the technology is purported to make murder a thing of the past. The watch bird is a flying policeman that monitors brain waves and can stop someone who is thinking of murder from committing it.

The watch birds are monitored by staff from the corporation that produces the technology. Initially, the rate of homicides in America drops to 62% and then to 50%. The watch birds have the power to think and learn about ways to ferret out murder. However, a flaw appears in the technology. A person is electrocuted by a watch bird after trying to strangle his wife. The bird should have simply immobilized the man – not killed him.

The corporation that makes and maintains the watch birds begins receiving reports that the birds are interfering with the normal process at slaughter houses by attacking workers slaughtering cattle. The birds are developing their own definition of murder. The company also receives reports that the birds won't permit fishing boats to go out to sea.

The technical people at the company want to adjust each watch bird when they return for maintenance. Watch birds begin stopping physicians from performing surgery and stop prisons from executing murderers. A watch bird comes to a house where the homemaker is trying to kill a moth. A man parking a car is killed by a watch bird when he turns off the engine. The birds believe the man had killed his automobile. Farmers won't plow their fields for fear the watch birds will think they are killing vegetation.

The president orders all watch birds grounded, but they begin attacking anyone trying to disable them. They believe they are living organisms compelled to protect themselves from being shot down. Without repairs, the birds will breakdown in six months. But the technologists think they can create a "hunter" watch bird to eliminate the regular watch birds in a time shorter than six months.

A "hawk" watch bird is developed. Some at the company think that the watch birds should simply be allowed to run down. But the hawk versions are released and start destroying the regular watch birds. Subsequently, a hawk goes berserk and kills humans. Now the technologists think that once all the watch birds are eliminated, the hawks will begin killing more humans.

People are afraid to go outside. Some at the company that created the birds theorize that the hawks will turn to killing each other if everyone stays inside. The president issues an order for everyone to shelter in place for three days. After three days, the skies are clear of hawks.

The Robert Sheckley story on which the radio play was based appeared in the February 1953 edition of *Galaxy* magazine. The radio episode was largely faithful to the story with a few exceptions. A company headed by Charles Gelsen is only one of seven facilities making watchbirds. The United States is divided into seven areas each to be supplied watchbirds by a manufacturer.

Criminologists have found that most murderers emit a different kind of brain wave from ordinary people. This finding was the basis for development of the technology. While the watchbirds don't initially stop all murders, they have been equipped with the ability to learn from each encounter and transmit their experience to other watchbirds leading to the problems addressed in the radio play.

As in the radio episode, a hawk is developed to shoot down the watchbirds. But the only solution to eliminating the hawks in the story seems to be developing new technology to kill the hawks once the hawks have done away with the watchbirds.

"Inside Earth" – February 26, 1953

Story: Poul Anderson

This radio broadcast is also one that has apparently been lost. It was based on a short story in the April 1951 issue of *Galaxy Science Fiction.* However, a script for the radio episode does exist.

The short story concerned the Valgolians conquering earth. Conru, a fifty-two-year-old Valgolian, disguised as an earthling, is chosen by General Vorka for a dangerous assignment. Rebellious earthlings are not making any progress unseating the Valgolians because of their internal differences among races and nationalities. The beings from Valgola are trying to help humans unite. Conru is tasked with getting humans to hate the beings from his planet so that earthlings will ignore their different racial and ethnic divisions and work together. The Valgolians seek to make humans hate them more than earthlings hate each other.

The Valgolians have already assisted a man named Levinsohn, a Jew, to lead a rebel group. Conru, using the name Conrad Haugen, poses as an earthling to infiltrate the League of Freedom, the main rebel group. He is able to go to the main rebel base where he falls in love with Barbara, a rebel leader. Conru learns that the rebels are planning an attack on the Valgolians, but he believes the rebels are not prepared enough for the attack to be successful. Trying to contact his commander, Conru causes the base's general alarm system to go off falsely alerting the rebels to an incoming attack. While everyone is preparing for the attack, Conru uses the time to contact Vorka to inform him of what the rebels are planning. The Valgolians then put down a premature rebel onslaught.

The Valgolians hope that the rebels, with each defeat, will learn something and, in the end, all races on earth will respect each other and work together to fight the Valgolians.

In the radio script, the series announcer, Omentor (Raymond Johnson) plays the lead role of Conru (aka Conrad Haugen), the Valgolian posing as an earthling. The character starts out as the foreman of a group of workers at a steel mill in New Chicago where he encounters Mike Reilly who puts him in contact with elements of the Legion of Freedom. From New Chicago, Conrad travels to the coast of Maine where he meets Nat Hawkins, another member of the group. Conrad undergoes a lie detector test to ensure that he is truly sympathetic to the Legion of Freedom's cause and then he is sent to Hood Island where he is introduced to Barbara Hood whose family had supposedly been killed by the Valgolians. Hood Island is the drop-off point from the rebels' main base to deliver weapons and propaganda about their cause. Harry Kane is a pilot for one of the space ships delivering material from the Legion of Freedom's base somewhere in the cosmos. Conrad is seeking its location to report to the Valgolians. Nat Hawkins, Barbara Hood, and Conrad are transported to the base since it is almost time for the rebels to mount their attack. The base is located on Boreas, a dead star. Conrad is put in charge of the alarm system on the base.

Barbara confides that the Legion of Freedom is in contact with the planet of Luron, the archenemies of the Valgolians, to assist them in their fight against the latter. By setting off a false alarm, Conrad is able to get in touch with Vorka to relay the location of the rebel base. Vorka sends a Supernova to bombard the rebels promising that no one will be killed. The Valgolians take out the rebels' surface installations and grounded space fleet but spare human life. The leading rebels and those judged potentially dangerous are taken to penal colonies which are really indoctrination centers where they are given a better understanding of the Valgolian Empire. Eventually, they will be returned to earth after their "forced evolution" learning to live in peace with other races and ethnic groups. In the indoctrination centers, Barbara will meet those of her family she thought had been killed by the Valgolians.

"The Moon Is Green" – March 5, 1953

Story: Fritz Leiber

Hank and Effie are married and living in a ground floor apartment. Hank sees Effie looking out a window at the moon. He orders her to close the shutters immediately and get away from the window. She describes the moon as green as a beer bottle, green as emeralds. Her husband responds that the shutters are not to be opened at least for the next five years. Hank then tells her to "count" herself.

She takes a Geiger counter and goes over her head and shoulders, her arms and back with the instrument. When she comes to her waist, the instrument begins clicking faster due to a wristwatch with a radium dial in her pocket.

The couple must stay indoors all the time ever since the great war decimated the earth with atomic weapons. Radiation from the bombs has drifted around the world for years. The air is alive with deadly radiation.

The two were only allowed to reclaim their ground-level apartment because the Committee believed them to be responsible people and because Hank has been making a good showing lately. If the Committee were to find that Effie was opening the lead shutters to look out the window, it would send both back to the lower levels of their building. Also, the Committee has been concerned about Effie's sterility. It was about to enter Hank's name on the list of those about to be allotted a free woman so Hank could produce offspring. But now, Effie is pregnant.

Hank and his wife are due to attend a banquet tonight since Hank is to become a member of the Junior Committee. Effie tells him to go to the banquet by himself since she is not feeling well. Hank responds that his wife should go to bed given her condition.

Hank leaves. Effie begins having ideas about looking through the window again to see if anything is alive outside. She opens the shutters and sees a man's face with full lips, large eyes, and a thin nose with no radiation welts or scars. Effie works the little crank to open the window and the man, named Patrick, comes into the apartment. She prepares some cold meat and canned bread for him and makes some coffee.

The man tells her that the earth has come back from the war's destruction and that it is now much better than it was before the apocalypse. There are flowers with large petals, stingless bees, and house cats as big as leopards. Children now have seven fingers on each hand and eight toes on each foot.

Hank unexpectedly returns to the apartment wearing a nose respirator and carrying an automatic pistol. Patrick says that he just happened by and knocked on the window, and Effie let him in. Hank replies that he knows why his wife is suddenly going to have a child after four long years. Patrick denies the accusation. Effie says that Hank should forget his silly jealousy and that Patrick has something wonderful to tell them. They no longer need to fear the radioactive dust. Everything outside has changed but changed for the better. They can go outside again.

Hank orders Patrick to use the Geiger counter to count himself. He does, and the clicks begin to chatter like a machine gun. Patrick says that he is indeed radioactive – that he is death itself, but the dust hasn't killed him yet. About the nice things he told Effie regarding the outside world, Patrick says it was just a line that he has found that women fall for. What is outside is just a little worse than either Hank or Effie can imagine.

Effie doesn't believe him. She thinks it is like a garden outside that he doesn't want to share with anyone. With a sudden pull, she jerks open the window, leaps to the sill, and hurries off into the darkness. Patrick goes out the window as well. Hank just stands there in the apartment. Finally, he closes the window and the lead shutters and takes up the Geiger counter to count himself.

The story appeared in the April 1952 edition of *Galaxy* magazine. No recording of the radio broadcast could be located.

"Martians Never Die" – March 12, 1953

Cast: Lesley Woods
George Petrie
Leon Janney
Lynn Cook
Story: Lucius Daniel

Since Dr. Clyde Curtis has been gone for five years, his wife contemplates having him declared dead. Hal Stern, a friend of Clyde's, helped the doctor finance his mission to Mars. Along with a young reporter, Stern and Mrs. Curtis await his return from the Red Planet. Stern has mixed feelings about the doctor's homecoming since, in the intervening years, he has fallen in love with the doctor's wife.

Curtis finally returns along with a special bodyguard named Schaughtowl. Schaughtowl hops like a frog, is five feet tall, and acts like a guard dog protecting the doctor. Dr. Curtis says that his bodyguard will not hurt a friend. Stern wants to tell the doctor that he has developed romantic feelings toward Mrs. Curtis. He also thinks of doing away with the doctor.

Dr. Curtis is examined by a physician who finds nothing wrong with him. Curtis says that Martians told him that he just needs a lot of rest to recover from his journey. Stern takes Curtis outside to rest beside a deep ravine in the back of the Curtis' house. Stern first wants to dispose of Schaughtowl, but the creature seems to be aware of Stern's intentions.

Dr. Curtis tells Stern that crime is virtually non-existent on Mars. Potential criminals are turned into their own victims. Stern picks up a rock and hits Schaughtowl on the back of its head. The creature goes over the ravine. Next Stern administers a stimulant to Clyde Curtis thinking that the doctor's heart will react in such a way to kill him. Curtis begins feeling warm and accuses Stern of killing Schaughtowl. He then says that Martians never really die – not even their animals.

"Martians Never Die" first appeared in the April 1952 edition of *Galaxy*. In general, the plot is the same as the radio episode. In the short story, the space craft in which Dr. Curtis returns to earth is a large sphere of metal alloy. Schaughtowl is described thusly upon its first appearance, "Something old and leathery and horrible was emerging from the circular doorway. Several tentacles, like so many snakes, slid around the hand rail which ran down the steps… It seemed…to combine the repulsive qualities of a spider and a toad."[38] The creature makes a gulping noise – "Gull Lup."

The ending of the story is also perhaps more fitting. Schaughtowl stings Stern's hand before Stern hits the creature with a rock and sends it tumbling into the ravine behind Dr. Curtis' house. The numbness from the sting begins to creep along Stern's right arm and to his right leg and then to his chest and neck. Stern begins to feel a strange sense of loyalty to Curtis. When Curtis tells Stern that he killed Schaughtowl, he begins to pet Stern like he had the creature from Mars. Stern responds "Gull Lup."

"The Girls from Earth" – March 19, 1953

Story: Frank M. Robinson

The year is 2906. Space travel has sent humans to every solar system possible to populate the planets. Most of the colonists have been men. On earth, there are ten women for every three men.

Karl and Joe are working in a sawmill on Mid-Planet in a galaxy far from earth. A ship is due from earth bringing some women as marriage prospects for the men on the planet. Joe and Karl know two women designated for them as numbers fifty-three and fifty-four. One of the women named Ruby chooses to go to Mid-Planet as an alternative to going to prison for shoplifting. The other woman whom Karl hopes to meet is named Phyllis.

Upon disembarking on Mid-Planet, Ruby sees Joe and loves his beard; Phyllis likes Karl's looks. Both couples go to the justice of the peace to get married and then visit their cabins by a river. The two women soon tire of the domestic chores they are tasked with such as washing their clothes in the river. They also dislike the large mosquitos and the three-month rainy season which leads to flooding. The two women decide to stow away on a space ship back to earth. However, the flooding is so bad, they attempt to return to their cabins but become lost. They are finally rescued by their husbands.

The short story in the January 1952 issue of *Galaxy* magazine focused mainly on the two men Karl Allen, a fur trapper, and Joe Hill, a sawmill operator and the three women who go to Mid-Planet looking for men. The three women are Ruby Johnson, thirty-two-years old who was caught shoplifting and given the choice of a long prison sentence or becoming a colonist; Phyllis Hanson, thirty, a typist who lives alone and answers an ad "Come to the Colonies, the Planets of Romance;" and Suzanne Carstens, who like Ruby, is given the choice of prison for soliciting or becoming a colonist.

Landing on Mid-Planet, Phyllis thinks that she has been sold a "bill of goods" upon seeing a collection of rundown shacks and corrugated huts. However, the men look healthy. As the women file out of the rocket, the men think they are glamorous. Unlike the radio episode, the short story does not describe what the women endured after they disembarked from the space ship.

"The Old Die Rich" – March 26, 1953

Cast: John Raby
Rolly Bester

Maurice Tarplin
Story: H. L. Gold

Mark Weldon learns that old people are dying of starvation although they have money in their bank accounts. He finds one such man is still alive, but, by the time he arrives at the hospital, the man is dead. The doctors believe the people dying had dementia and that is why they starve to death despite having money to buy food. The deceased have no identification on them. An analysis of the ink in their bank books looks new. The most recent man who passed away mumbled something about a Miss Roberts before he died.

Mark finds a May Roberts who placed a newspaper ad directed at elderly men. He makes himself up as an old man and goes to meet her. However, he mistakenly gives her his references and Social Security Number which leads to him initially deemed unqualified by Miss Roberts for her project. The other responders to the ad had no Social Security Numbers.

He returns later and breaks into her house. Roberts knows what Mark is investigating. She is the daughter of a physicist and a physicist herself. She shows Mark her laboratory which has a time machine. She orders him to undress and put on clothes from twenty years ago.

Roberts forces Mark into the time machine and gives him various envelopes to open in a certain sequence. Mark finds himself in 1931, on May 15. The envelopes contain money and instruct him to deposit some in a bank, buy stock with other money, and bet on sporting events for which she knows the outcome. Mark is then returned to 1953. Roberts tells Mark that the purpose of the machine is to help all mankind by saving the world which otherwise would be destroyed.

Roberts now wants to send Mark into the future to find a box that contains enough energy to run an entire city. She sends him to the year 2023 to gather technical information to build such a box since the physical box cannot be brought back from the future. The machine will only return what was transported in the first place.

Mark finds himself in a city where he locates an electrical appliance store which has a box called a "Dynapack." He asks a stranger for information about a Dynapack. The stranger knows that he is Mark Weldon from the twentieth century. The stranger also is aware of May Roberts and why Mark is there. The man turns out to be the city's mayor and takes Mark to his house where he is given a meal of canned foodstuffs from the twentieth century. He is told that if he were to eat fresh food, he would die like the old men who passed away since eating fresh food from the twenty-first century would be an alien object which could not be transported back by the time machine. The mayor says that May thought Mark would die like the other men when he returns to 1953. According to her papers that the mayor has read, May wants to use the technical information about the Dynapack to enslave people in her time and not to benefit all mankind. She is seeking revenge for how people had treated her father.

When Mark returns to 1953, May finds that he is not dying of starvation. She threatens Mark with a gun. He gets the upper hand, forces her into the time machine, and sends her to the year 2023. The police arrest Mark for her murder but, since no body can be found, he is released. Mark ends up with $15,000 from his investments that he made in 1931.

The short story, published in the March 1953 issue of *Galaxy* magazine, is similar to the radio episode. It clarifies that Mark Weldon is a twenty-five-year-old actor who is prematurely bald and often plays roles of elderly men. He believes that, if he can learn why old people starve to death while leaving a small fortune, he could turn the story into a play and make a name for himself.

After Mark travels to the future in search of the Dynapack, the story differs from the radio show. After visiting the appliance store, Weldon leaves and hides out in a primary school where he views films about the history of exploration of the Solar System and developments in medicine, architecture, and history. A woman enters the room and asks if she can help him. He quickly leaves and hides in the school's basement.

At night, Mark leaves the school building looking for something to eat. He meets a man named Carr who takes him to a restaurant where he is given only dehydrated food from his time period. At the restaurant, Leo Blandell introduces himself as the chairman of the Mark Weldon Committee who made sure Weldon felt comfortable upon his arrival in the future. The people in the city knew that Mark was arriving from reading papers left behind by May Roberts and so had prepared for his appearance. Mark is informed that he will stay a month in the future.

When Weldon returns to his time period after a month, May asks him for the notes about the Dynapack. He shoots her in the right arm. She drops the derringer she was holding to kill him. He tells her that the people from the future knew he was coming. Mark forces May into the time machine. The rest of the story ends like the radio episode.

"Morrow on Mars" – April 2, 1953

Cast: George Petrie
Fran Carlon
Leon Janney

The year is 4000 A D, the place, Mars. Matt Morrow, the editor of the *Mars News*, a tele paper, is visited by Professor Rinker who has traveled from earth on a space rocket. The professor is a little, frightened man wearing a blue surge suit and a straw hat covering his hearing aid. The professor tells Morrow that Mars is wobbling on its axis. He shows Morrow his wristwatch which floats in the air. When Morrow receives a call from his wife, the professor disappears.

Matt goes home to his wife, Gwen, and takes the professor's watch with him. It is made of trineutrium, a very precious mineral found only on Mars. The little man wanted to tell Morrow about the mineral. The police call Morrow and report that the professor has been speaking with Sedgwick, the head of the trineutrium mining concern.

Morrow and his wife head to the mine fields where Matt talks with Sedgwick about the professor. The professor told Sedgwick that someone is trying to steal the valuable mineral. Morrow goes back to his wife and, on the way, finds the professor who says that he was tied up by space thieves. The professor also says that thieves are using a special process to lighten trineutrium to make it easier to transport to earth. By reducing the weight of the mineral, the weight of Mars is also reduced which is why the planet is wobbling.

The thieves approach Morrow and the professor. The two attempt to get away from them but are eventually captured. When Morrow opens his eyes, he discovers that he and the professor are strapped to chairs inside a space craft. Sedgwick is the leader of the thieves. The ship blasts off to earth.

Sedgwick plans to jettison Morrow and the professor into space, but first he puts them in space suits with twenty-four-hours' worth of oxygen. The two are ejected. Eventually, a rocket ship from Mars with the police and Mrs. Morrow save them. Morrow's wife had overheard what Sedgwick was planning. The professor's hearing aid under his straw hat served as a tracking device for the police to locate them.

The police along with the Morrow's and the professor then go after Sedgwick and his crew. When they land on earth, the Mars police are waiting for them.

This episode seems to be an original work for the radio series. No corresponding story could be found in any issue of *Galaxy* magazine.

"The Drop" – April 9, 1953

Story: Samuel Christopher Youd (under the pseudonym John Christopher)

As with several other episodes of the radio series, no recording of this presentation could be found. However, the short story on which the radio episode is based was published in the March 1953 edition of *Galaxy Science Fiction*.

The tale involves thirty-four-year-old Jake Newsam, the commander of a space ship who arrives at Forbeston on Mars. After a nuclear holocaust on earth, surviving humans moved to other planets in the solar system where they live under domes in artificial environments. Nonetheless, anyone deemed a misfit by the Directorate, the government entity overseeing all the human colonies, is sent back to earth.

On Mars, Newsam is looking for a friend named Larry Gaines, a fellow space ship commander. He visits Gaines' home but finds no one there and the furniture covered in dust. Two men in medical uniforms enter Gaines' house and ask Newsam to undergo a medical check-up even though he just had one. They forcibly take him to the Medical Building and place him under a Verifier to question him about what he knows about various space ship commanders. He is released. The Medical Captain refuses to tell him why he was picked up and questioned.

Newsam goes to the Persepolis Club to ask about his friend Gaines, but no one has seen him recently. Matthews, another space ship commander, tells Newsam that Gaines had been classified as a misfit and dropped to earth. Newsam responds that Gaines was perfectly sane when he last saw him. Matthews says that Gaines was classified 3-K meaning he participated in organized activities against the State.

Matthews is part of a group whose objective is to overthrow the current government. They seek to go back to earth and recolonize the planet – to lead a natural life in natural surroundings and not live within artificial environments on other planets. When Gaines' membership in the group was discovered, he was dropped to North America.

Matthews tells Newsam that the group wants to bring Gaines back from earth. He asks Newsam to become a misfit and be dropped to earth to find Gaines. Newsam volunteers for the mission and is scheduled to be sent back to earth. Nevertheless, he undergoes a final interrogation after being given drugs by the State where it finds out about Matthews' plans for Newsam.

Newsam is dropped in what used to be New Hampshire. Gaines locates his friend when he hits the ground. Larry Gaines tells Newsam that the story Matthews had relayed was not correct because the group knew that misfits receive a final interrogation before being dropped. Also, earth is no longer a radioactive wasteland as portrayed by the State.

On earth, there are villages connecting small, scattered buildings that are camouflaged to make it difficult for the government on Mars to discern them through a telescope. Newsam is informed that Matthews will soon be joining him on earth.

Appendix: *Out There* – CBS' Answer to *Tales of Tomorrow*

Premiering October 28, 1951 on CBS Sundays at 6:00 pm, less than three months after *Tales of Tomorrow* debuted on ABC, *Out There* was created by Donald Davis, produced by John Baggott, and directed by Byron Paul and Andrew McCullough. It was a science fiction series that appealed to both adults and children. Each episode combined live action with filmed special effects. Stories were generally adapted from the works of leading science fiction writers.

Extraterrestrials

The debut episode of *Out There* was based on a short story by Graham Doar about mankind's first encounter with a flying saucer. Called "The Outer Limit," the story told of U.S. Air Force rocket ship pilot, Captain Bill Hurley, being captured in space by Commander Xegion (Wesley Addy) of the "Intergalactic Council." The Commander sends Captain Hurley back to earth with the message that unless earthlings cease atomic war preparations, the Intergalactic Council will destroy the planet. Since no one believes the captain's story, Xegion's crew is on the verge of annihilating earth. However, Hurley's ten-year-old son speaks up and says that he does believe. Earthlings are given another chance. The inhabitants of the other worlds are waiting to see what the younger generation of people on earth will do.

"The Outer Limit" was first published in the December 24, 1949 issue of *The Saturday Evening Post.* The television adaptation goes beyond the original story. In the original, Bill, flying an experimental jet, traveling at least four times the speed of sound, notes a metallic object ahead of him. Search planes begin looking for Bill and his aircraft to no avail. The search goes on for hours and then a colonel named Hank receives a report that Bill has landed.

The colonel asks Bill how he stretched ten minutes of fuel to keep the jet in the air for over ten hours. Bill responds that he chased a flying saucer and that he has been tipped off as to how the world will end. He then blacked out. When he regained consciousness, he was surrounded by space aliens. The aliens telecommunicated thoughts to him.

A psychiatrist joins the colonel in the debriefing. The aliens are knowledgeable of the uses and dangers of atomic power. They have sealed off earth from the rest of space because of earthlings' experiments with atomic bombs. The aliens have spread a layer one hundred miles above earth. When an atomic bomb explodes, the radioactive particles rise and infiltrate the layer. After the radioactivity in the layer rises above the normal level of cosmic activity, the particles will begin fission and explosions will occur causing the end of the world.

The colonel and the psychiatrist do not believe Bill's story. The aliens, however, report the results of their encounter with Bill to their sector commander.

The outline for "Seven Temporary Moons," the December 16, 1951 episode of the series, opens with bulbous, not-streamlined, unhuman spacecrafts sweeping across earth's skies. Newspaper headlines read: "Seven Temporary Moons Are Space-Ships, Says Army!" The story was written by William Jenkins under the pseudonym Murray Leinster.

In an observatory manned by Murfee and Burton, the two are attempting to use a special telescope and a gimcrack device attached to an astronomical camera to photograph the space ships. The gimcrack device was made by Bud Gregory whom Burton calls a "country bumpkin" but whom Murfee says is a genius ever since Bud repaired a spectroheliograph using a bottle cap and two pieces of aluminum wire.

The alien space crafts are surveying earth to decide whether to tame mankind or simply wipe it out before taking over the planet. Murfee takes a photo of one of the space ships to show Bud who lives in a cabin in the wilderness. Murfee explains to him that the space ships plan to attack earth. The aliens are using a tractor beam to snatch large items from earth for their inspection. Murfee would like to create a large tractor beam to grab a space craft, drag it down to earth, and smash it. He wants Gregory's help in creating such a beam, but Gregory isn't interested.

Murfee decides to show Gregory's sixteen-year-old daughter, Letty, a mail-order catalog and tells her to begin crying in front of her dad over what she wants to purchase from the catalog with funds Gregory will earn from creating a tractor beam. Gregory begins working on the device. Murfee also wants him to create a pressor beam. Combined, the two beams will pull at iron and push at aluminum, pull at carbon and push at steel so that every possible form of agitation will be produced to destroy the alien ships.

Murfee works on turning a big empty oil tank into a space ship to fly into orbit with the gadgets Gregory is developing. He has Gregory with him as the homemade space craft takes off. Murfee advises Gregory that a tractor beam from the aliens is heading toward the observatory and Gregory's cabin. The gadgets blow up the alien craft one-by-one. Murfee's space ship makes it back to earth.

In the end, Murfee says, "Look, Bud, you get that mail-order catalog away from Letty and pick yourself out a nice new fishing-rod. I'll pay for it. And don't worry about my telling anybody that we saved the world! Nobody'd believe me, anyhow!"[39]

Space Exploration

Several episodes of *Out There* were based on stories by Robert Heinlein. Heinlein was one of the first science fiction writers to have his stories published in mainstream magazines in the 1940s such as *The Saturday Evening Post.* He emphasized scientific accuracy in his fiction and published books like *Stranger in a Strange Land* and *Starship Troopers.*

"Ordeal in Space," airing November 4, 1951, was the first Heinlein short story, written under the pseudonym Ralph Sloan, to be presented on *Out There.*

The original story focused on William Cole, Chief Communications Officer and relief pilot for the rocket ship, Valkyrie, a passenger liner on the Earth-Moon to Mars route. As the ship is approaching the Mars Terminal on Deimos, a Martian satellite, it loses its primary piloting radar. The space craft is revolving on its axis to provide artificial gravity for its passengers. William Cole is tasked with a spacewalk to fix the problem. As he proceeds from the ship, he falls into outer space and is not rescued for two hours when he is picked up by another craft.

The incident leaves him with acrophobia. He is grounded and seeks psychiatric help. Changing his name to William Saunders, he lands a job calibrating electronic equipment for a small firm that makes custom-built communication systems. In the new job, he becomes friends with Joe Tully who invites him for dinner at his high-rise apartment. He stays overnight. Late at night, Bill hears a kitten on a ledge protruding below the window on the thirty-fifth floor. He decides to rescue it. He is able to pick the kitten up off the high-rise ledge and is cured of his acrophobia.

The second Heinlein story to air on the series was "Misfit" (November 18, 1951). This story focused on A.J. Libby, nicknamed "Pinkie," a recruit to the Space Marines on a mission to asteroid AS 5388G to build Space Station E-M3. When the space craft arrives at its destination, the Marines put on space suits before embarking. Libby turns out to be a mathematical genius. When assigned to a roofing detail as part of an effort to build a permanent campsite, he corrects some math errors related to the construction.

The biggest mission of the Marines is to determine how to push the asteroid out of its orbit and move it to a new orbit between earth and Mars. Explosive charges will be set at various places on the asteroid to accomplish this.

Libby points out that a mistake has been made on the size of an explosive charge. When the Marine supervising the operation doesn't believe Libby, Libby pulls out the electrodes attached to the explosive device before it can detonate. The supervisor goes over his calculations with Libby and realizes he was not correct.

Subsequently, Captain Doyle, in charge of the entire mission, tests Libby's knowledge of mathematics which show Libby is a genius. Libby can give the captain precise calculations of final explosions when a machine designed to do the computations breaks down. The mission is successful in changing the asteroid's orbit.

"The Green Hills of Earth" (December 2, 1951) was also supposedly based on a Heinlein short story about a character named Rhysling, a blind singer of the space ways. He had been a spaceman on the Goshawk that was powered by atomic energy. Rhysling had been fired, backlisted, and grounded for having spent his time writing a song when he should have been watching his gauges. Nevertheless, the attrition of spacemen caused him to be given another chance. He had been blinded from a blue radioactive glow in the power room of his ship when trying to repair one of the ship's engines.

After becoming blind, he imagined things as he thought they should be. All women were beautiful; all men were gracious. His singing brought him donations from his audience. He composed "The Green Hills of Earth" before he was blinded. The final verse of the song went:

> "We pray for one last landing
> On the globe that gave us birth;
> Let us rest my eyes on the fleecy skies
> And the cool, green hills of Earth."

Apparently, Raphael Hayes, who wrote the television episode, only used the title of Heinlein's story. However, as Alan Morton points out in his book, *The Golden Age of Telefantasy*, the actual episode, according to the CBS press release, dealt with a research party led by a female biologist who sets out to explore the recently discovered Wolf Pack asteroids.[40]

"The Sense of Wonder" (November 11, 1951), an original short story by Milton Lesser, focused on Rikud, a twenty-five-year-old man who has been on a space ship all his life. His daily activities include taking a bath in health-rays and watching the changeless sweep of space from the ship's viewport. Rikud knows that, when he becomes thirty, he would be allowed to have children and that when he reaches one hundred he will die. He notes that the stars in the sky seem to be changing but "change" and "variability" are two words without meaning. One of the biggest and brightest stars he sees begins to grow larger. As it does, the roar in the rear of his world suddenly ceases. There is silence broken by sharp booming. Out of the viewport, he can see nothing but a cloud of white vapor. The vapor departs, and Rikud can see gardens rearward in his world. For an entire week, the view does not change. He continues to see a garden larger than his entire world of the spaceship.

Rikud has always wondered about the door in the back of the spaceship's library. He opens the door and sees a small room which has another door at the far end. A voice announces that no unauthorized persons can go through that door. The announcement goes on to say, "... this ship is a perfect, self-sustaining world. It is more than that: it is human-sustaining as well. Try to hurt yourself and the ship will not permit it - within limits, of course. But you can damage the ship, and to avoid any possibility of that, no unauthorized persons are to be permitted through this door – "[41]

Confused by the announcement, Rikud opens the second door anyway and sees cogs and gears and wheels and unknown other things all strange and beautiful. Rikud spies a third door which leads to a tunnel which in turn leads to another door which, after opening it, has a smaller version of the viewport. Out of the window, Rikud sees more of the garden with a ridge of mounds off in the distance. Out of this door, he can enter the garden, but Rikud is afraid to open it. Days go by. Finally, he decides to open the door after he has disabled the ship's machinery which results in the craft's inhabitants no longer automatically receiving food and water. He steps outside into the warmth and breathes air fresher than any air he has ever breathed. All the men and the women who reside in separate quarters join him. Rikud feels at home. It is much better than the small world of machinery, frightening doors, and women by appointment only.

Milton Lesser (1928-2008) wrote science fiction, mysteries, and fictional autobiographies under a variety of pseudonyms including Ellery Queen.

"The Man," the original story by Ray Bradbury which was adapted by Howard Rodman for the December 23, 1951 presentation, concerned a rocket from earth landing on a distant planet. Captain Hart, the commanding officer of the craft, wonders why no welcoming committee from the nearby city has come to greet his crew given that his rocket is the first ever to land on the planet. Martin, his lieutenant, learns that the space craft landed at an inopportune time. Something happened yesterday in the city – a remarkable man had appeared for whom the residents had watched for thousands of years. The man had healed the sick and comforted the poor.

The Captain, Martin, and other crew walk into the city. The mayor meets them. Hart believes that the residents of the city have been subjected to a mass hallucination. He demands specifics about what the man looked like and wants to question those who were healed by the man. His lieutenant criticizes the Captain for not believing that the man actually appeared. Martin says that he will not be returning on the rocket. Instead, he will stay in the city.

The Captain believes that the man who appeared was a fellow astronaut named Burton who landed on the planet ahead of him to establish oil and mineral rights under the guise of religion.

The astronauts return to their rocket and receive a report that two other space ships are coming – Burton's and Shipley's. A man from one of the ships, suffering severe burns, says that the two ships had been caught in a cosmic storm – only three men survived. Hart is surprised that Burton's ship had not landed on the planet earlier.

The Captain and his men return to the city to the mayor's auditorium to hear the man speak. Hart admits that he made a mistake about the man. He insists that the mayor tell him where the man is going. When the mayor doesn't, Hart shoots, wounding him. Hart wants to take his ship to go after the man. Martin travels back with Hart and the remaining crew to the rocket. Martin, along with some other crew members, intend to stay on the planet. Before Hart and the other crew leave, Martin asks him what he will say to the man if he ever finds him. Hart says he'll ask for a little peace and quiet. The mayor says that the Captain will search forever for the man not realizing that the man is still on the planet in the city.

"Susceptibility" (November 25, 1951) was adapted by David Shaw from a story by John D. MacDonald.

The opening scene takes place in a windowless room with a dispatcher sitting at a glass desk directing launches of spacecraft. Malloy, a young pilot, appears in the room ready for duty. His mission is to travel to Able XII in the third galaxy, and he will have one passenger. Malloy asks why a pilot is needed for a trip that can be reached with an automatic space craft. The dispatcher says that he may have other duties once he reaches his destination. The last pilot who went to the space station has not been heard from and no communication has been received from the experimental station.

Kuna, a scientist, is Malloy's passenger. He designed Able XII which he says is the most important experimental station of the whole colonial program. One thousand pioneers were sent thirty years ago to the station with another 25,000 scheduled to be sent shortly.

Reaching the station, Borg, Fellina, and Kark are at the command post of the space station. They are all lethargic not wanting to get out of their chairs even to order food or open the gate to allow others to enter. Kuna wonders where everyone else is. Fellina, the one female of the group, says that the others live far away from the automated center. Kuna and Malloy go looking for the leader – Deen Thomason, a female.

They find her living in her own cottage. Kuna says that the colonists were not supposed to have their own homes. Thomason replies that the colonists did not like the specific plans that Kuna had devised for them. Kuna relieves Deen of her duties and places her under arrest with Malloy watching her. Kuna leaves to prepare the space station on the planet for the 25,000 new colonists.

Deen indicates that, having worked to establish her cottage by chopping wood among other tasks, she is stronger than Malloy. She wants to demonstrate her strength by leaving and throws Malloy halfway across the room.

The next day, Deen prepares a large breakfast for Malloy. To Malloy, it doesn't make sense for Deen to work so much when she could have everything she needs simply by pushing a button. A few days pass, and Malloy thinks he will need treatment when he leaves the planet. He has a certain susceptibility which must be tracked down and eliminated because he enjoys working. Deen responds that, while machines have advanced over the years, humans have not since they don't need to think anymore in an automated world. She says that it is up to people like her to fight the Colonial Bureau. Malloy wants Deen to escape rather than encounter the wrath of the Bureau when they take her back. Malloy says that he will go back to the Center if she won't escape.

At the Center, Fellina, Borg, and Kark continue to doze with nothing to do except push buttons. Kuna threatens to report them for inefficiency. He informs them that he has contacted the Bureau and that the 25,000 new colonists are on their way. Malloy, having returned to the Center, is told by Kuna what buttons to press to prepare for the incoming new residents.

Malloy returns to Deen and realizes that she is right about life and that he is in love with her. He tells Kuna that he is not going back. Kuna pulls a neutronic valve from his pocket capable of blowing up the entire planet. Deen takes the weapon from him. Kuna returns to the Center to be with the three others. They tell him that the exits from the Center are now locked because it is a prison.

The final episode of *Out There*, "The Castaway," aired January 13, 1952. The story, written by Nelson Bond, focused on the crew of a spaceship with Captain Bartlett at the helm and Lieutenant Wally Braitt as his assistant. They rescue a man in a spacesuit on an asteroid. The man's name is Paul Moran who has been missing for two years. Moran says that he was marooned on the asteroid by the crew from another space craft and that he is cursed. Bad things happen on space ships on which he is a passenger. Suddenly, equipment failures begin to take place on Bartlett's craft such as communication issues, refrigeration breakdowns, electrical problems, etc. Moran pleads with the crew to be put off the spaceship. Moran also confides to Braitt that Martians - not earthlings, were the first to explore space and that he is over 2000 years old. When the space craft's navigation system goes out, Moran calculates the ship's speed to save it from hitting the moon. Moran prays for his own death. Braitt tells the captain that Moran is really John Cartephilas – one of the greatest physicists of all time. Bartlett attempts to convince Moran to prevent the spaceship from crashing to end Moran's life. Moran has an epiphany and changes his mind about crashing the ship. The craft lands safely on earth, but Moran disappears from the craft. Cartephilas, the wandering Jew, after showing mercy to the crew, was able to die.

Space Aliens among Us

Written by Edward Waldo (Theodore Sturgeon), "Mewhu's Jet" was the December 9, 1951 installment of the series.

At night, something hits Jack Garry's vacation cottage by the sea. His young daughter finds a man with silver-gray skin and a broken arm who whimpers. Jack's wife places the broken arm in a splint.

The next day, the man begins communicating with Jack and his daughter using a strange accent. Mewhu also communicates with the daughter through mental telepathy. Molly, the daughter, takes her dad into the nearby woods where Mewhu is standing beside a tree. Way up in the tree is a gleaming object. Jack retrieves the object and finds that it has capabilities of working like a parachute to prevent someone from crashing to the ground and also works like a pogo stick to allow someone to ascend off the ground. The object has small jet engines on either side along with rings to hold a person's arms. Mewhu demonstrates a motor inside the pogo-chute which Jack can use in cutting wood to repair the roof of the cottage that was destroyed by Mewhu's craft the previous night.

After completing the roof repairs, Jack takes Mewhu to visit the manager of the local airport. While talking with the manager, Mewhu gets out of Jack's car and runs toward the hanger area where he gets inside a light aircraft. The plane takes off, but, not being familiar with the aircraft, Mewhu crashes it. Mewhu is taken to the hospital where the doctor doesn't know how to treat him given his strange anatomy. Eventually, Mewhu recovers. Based on Mewhu's actions while on earth, Jack concludes that Mewhu is really a child from another planet who commandeered a spaceship and accidentally landed on earth. The alien will not be able to explain in detail his planet any more than a six-year-old human being can explain the biology, the physics, and other facts of earth.

"The Bus to Nowhere" (December 30, 1951), written by Reginald Rose, focuses on strangers on a stalled bus at 3:00 am in the middle of the Mojave Dessert. In addition to the driver, the passengers are Jack and Helen, a young couple; Mac, a heavy set, fast-talking man; Bill, a young soldier; and Harry and Sue. The bus driver announces that they are stuck for the night and that it feels like something outside is holding the bus in place.

Mr. Kik, a small, elderly man, slowly climbs onto the bus. He is dressed very warmly in an overcoat, hat, and muffler. He purchases a ticket and, when the driver gives him his change, Kik's hands feel like ice. The driver explores outside the bus. The passengers hear a crackling noise like an electrical arc jumping between two poles. The driver tells the passengers that there is something outside that tears a person apart. Subsequently, Sue discovers that the bus driver is dead.

Mr. Kik stands in front of the door as if he is guarding everyone. Bill wants to go outside, but Kik will not allow him. He tells the passengers that it would be dangerous for them to walk more than five feet from the bus in any direction. He also says that he is responsible for the passengers and that the driver's death was an object lesson to keep everyone on the bus. He challenges the passengers to walk down the steps of the bus with their hands outstretched. When they feel their hands touch something, they should immediately go back inside the bus. Mac is the first one to meet the challenge. A crackling noise is heard. Mac screams and is helped back by Bill. Kik says that the bus is incapsulated by something like a magnetic band.

Kik reveals that he has been in the United States for about three years and came from Venus on a space ship. Furthermore, he says that all the passengers are about to disappear from earth and travel to Venus. A space ship is due to appear at any moment. Bill grabs a gun that Mac had retrieved from the bus driver and shoots Kik but doesn't harm him in any way. Kik says that his body is constructed so that simple wounds heal almost immediately and that beings from Venus are cold-blooded because of the hot temperatures on the planet.

Kik says that earthlings are on the brink of destroying themselves and their planet and that scientists on Venus want to know why. The bus passengers are to be examined by the scientists on Venus.

The space ship from Venus is coming. Mac seizes a nearby fire extinguisher and sprays Mr. Kik. Bill grabs a fire axe. starts to hack at Kik's body, and kills him. Mac then instructs the rest to leave the bus one at a time and hug the outside of the bus. Sue suggests that one of them try to flee to warn the world about the beings from Venus. They wait for the spaceship to remove the barrier around the bus. The passengers fight with the space men from Venus while Sue sprints away and flags down a car driven by state troopers. She tells the troopers about the space craft and what happened to the other passengers. The troopers don't seem to believe her. She feels their hands which are as cold as ice.

Reginald Rose is probably best remembered for writing the play *Twelve Angry Men* and for creating the television series, *The Defenders*. However, his first writing credit for television was the episode described above.

A Matter of Time

The short story "Guest in the House" (January 6, 1952), written by Frank Belknap Long begins, "Roger Shevlin sets down his bags, shook the rain from his umbrella and wondered just how long it would be before he found himself consulting a psychiatrist." Roger has rented a twenty-room house and has "renter's remorse."[42] He moves his wife Elsie and his two youngsters into the home. The previous tenant, a physics professor, left some machinery in the cellar. Roger descends the stairs to the basement, touches the machinery which seems to vibrate for a while, and something seems to lift him off the floor.

Upstairs his wife claims that a fine, drizzling mist surrounds the house. She sees a little man with a horrible, shrunken face looking at her though a window. Roger ascends the stairs. Going out the front door, he sees the little man who introduces himself as "Papenek." Papenek says that Shevlin has discovered the secret to time travel. When the machinery in the basement started, the house traveled in time and now is a half million years in the future. Papenek then transports himself into the house through its outer wall using a lighted tube that he possesses. He informs Roger that a Great Holocaust caused by a nuclear war wiped out most of humanity. The remaining humans began to mutate in the subsequent 500,000 years and now look like him.

Shevlin reveals to Papenek that he didn't invent time travel - that it was all an accident. The little man says that he may be able to figure out how the machinery in the cellar works and, if so, Roger and his family can be transported back in time to when they moved into their current dwelling. While Papenek attempts to figure out the machinery, he will be the Shevlin's house guest.

Papenek begins working on the machine. After three days, Roger is becoming impatient with his house guest. He grasps Papenek's glowing tube from him as the little man tells him that he has found a way to send the house back in time. He explains how to manipulate the equipment to make that happen. Roger forces Papenek out of the house using the glowing tube as Roger's son, who turns out to be a child prodigy, works the machinery. After a sudden dazzling flash of light, presumably the house returns to the moment the Shevlin family moved in.

Frank Belknap Long (1901-1994) authored several works in a large variety of genres from science fiction to poetry. In 1978, Long was honored with the World Fantasy Award for Life Achievement.

Out There was under consideration by CBS to be revived in 1952 to compete against NBC's ratings hit, *The Milton Berle Show* but that didn't happen.

Endnotes

1 Jay Allen Sanford, "Tales of Tomorrow: The Inside Story of TV's 1st Sci-Fi Anthology," *San Diego Reader*, April 25, 2020, retrieved November 29, 2021.

2 Val Adams, "The World of the Future Comes to Television," *The New York Times*, September 23, 1951.

3 Robert F. Lewine, "Why Film Was Rejected for 'Tales of Tomorrow,' *Television Magazine*, July 1952, 21.

4 "Tales on Film," at Deadline, *Broadcasting*, September 21, 1953.

5 Sidney Field, "My Nephew Norvell" Script, Nelson Bond Collection, Marshall University, undated.

6 Adams, "The World of the Future," September 23, 1951.

7 Ibid.

8 Jay Allen Sanford, "Tales of Tomorrow."

9 Russell V. Ritchey, "What would you do?," *Collier's*, June 26, 1948, 28.

10 J.C. May, "Dune Roller," *Astounding Science Fiction,* December 1951, 43.

11 Quoted in Jay Allen Sanford, "Tales of Tomorrow," *San Diego Reader*, April 25, 2020.

12 Jack Gould, "Radio and Television," *The New York Times*, February 4, 1952.

13 Merrill Panitt, "Screening TV," *The Philadelphia Inquirer*, April 2, 1952.

14 Quoted in Jay Allen Sanford, "Tales of Tomorrow," *San Diego Reader*, April 25, 2020.

15 Ibid.

16 Irving Robbin, "Space Interviews," Internet Archive Wayback Machine, December, 1999, retrieved April 21, 2023.

17 Contract for *Tales of Tomorrow*, Florence Anglin Papers, Billy Rose Division, New York Public Library, May 28 1952.

18 Alan Morton, "Tales of Tomorrow," *The Golden Age of Telefantasy: A Comprehensive Guide to Science Fiction, Fantasy and Horror Television Series of the 1940s and 1950s*, Bartonville, Illinois: Other World Books, 2020, 174.

19 Alfred Coppel, "The Exile," *Astounding Science Fiction*, October, 1952. 69.

20 Arthur C. Clarke, *The Collected Stories of Arthur C. Clarke*, New York: Tom Doherty Associates, 2000, 407.

21 Quoted in Jay Allen Sanford, "Tales of Tomorrow," *San Diego Reader*, April 25, 2020.

22 "Interplanetary Denizen Appears," *The Cincinnati Post*, September 6, 1952.

23 Quoted in Jay Allen Sanford, "Tales of Tomorrow," *San Diego Reader*, April 25, 2020.

24 Ibid.

25 Ibid.

26 Phyllis Sterling Smith, "The Quaker Lady and the Jelph," *Thrilling Wonder Stories*, August 1952, 113.

27 John Crosby, "Radio & Television," *The Charlotte News*, December 30, 1952.

28 Susan McKenzie, Private communication with author, May 17, 2023.

29 Irving Robbin, "Space Interviews."

30 Jack Gould, "Television in Review," *The New York Times*, February 16, 1953.

31 Jack Barden & Irwin Blacker, "Lonely Village," Irwin Blacker Papers, American Heritage Center, University of Wyoming.

32 Ibid.

33 Ibid.

34 See for instance, Alan Morton, *The Golden Age of Telefantasy*, 178.

35 Walter de la Mare, *The Wind Blows Over*, London: Faber and Faber Limited, 28.

36 Quoted in Val Adams, "The World of the Future Comes to Television," *The New York Times*.

37 Theodore Sturgeon, "The Stars Are the Styx," *Galaxy Science Fiction*, October 1950, 72.

38 Lucius Daniel, "Martians Never Die," *Galaxy Science Fiction*, April 1952, 108.

39 Murray Leinster, "The Seven Temporary Moons" Outline, Murray Leinster Papers, Syracuse University Libraries, undated.

40 Alan Morton, *The Golden Age of Telefantasy*, 117.

41 Milton Lesser, "The Sense of Wonder," *Galaxy Science Fiction*, September 1951.

42 Frank Belknap Long, "Guest in the House," *The Rim of the Unknown*, New York: Condor, 1962, 77.

Index